IT'S ONLY AN HOUR
A WEEK

IT'S ONLY AN HOUR A WEEK

Stories of ghosts, campfires and dirty little boys

Lawrence Bernstein

Third Printing, November, 2013

Cover art by Lynn M. Nattress

ISBN 978-1-62050-346-1

Printed in the United States of America

Larberns Press   Mount Prospect, Illinois

iv

To all the boys whose lives have touched

mine and who have left their

footprints on my heart

vi

Foreword

If you are about to read *It's Only an Hour a Week* you undoubtedly were or are presently involved in Scouting. Yes, magic does happen in the Scouting Program. How? You start with a small lad attending his first pack or troop meeting. He is probably a little apprehensive, but doesn't want to show it. Mom has bought a uniform a couple of sizes too large so he can grow into it, and thus "things" are rolled up and tucked in. His eyes are full of mischief and his pockets are full of "stuff." You watch over the years as this little kid becomes a mature, contributing young adult. The process happens like magic! It is a Scout Leader like Larry Bernstein, and thousands of others like him, who perform this magical process of turning the youth of today into the leaders of tomorrow (and enjoy doing it).

Like Larry, I strongly believe that the Boy Scouts of America has the best program available for the development of character, citizenship and physical and mental fitness for our youth. Developing leadership skills and instilling ethical values are areas in which the Scouting Program excels. Read on as Larry relates his experiences in Scouting. As you read, you'll feel the challenges, the humor, the frustrations and the rewards of working with kids (don't miss the chapter on how to turn off the rain).

So make yourself a big cup of hot chocolate (the real stuff, with milk and chocolate syrup), kick off your shoes, lean back in your favorite easy chair, and smell the wood smoke as you enjoy reading *It's Only an Hour a Week*. And when you finish, you might just want to contact your neighborhood Scout troop and ask to tag along as an assistant on their next campout – you'll never regret it.

Jim Boeger, Author
The Scoutmaster and
The Scoutmaster II

Acknowledgements

Thanks to my children, Randy, Michelle, Scott, Jim and Ken, without whose Scouting adventures there would have been no story to tell.

Thank you to all of my friends and relatives who have patiently listened to me ramble on about this book for the past seven years. Many of them were gracious enough to read it in its rawest form and encourage me to keep writing.

A very special thank you to my dear friend, Lois Sorkin, who re-connected my split infinitives and rescued my dangling participles. If it were not for her mastery of language, this book would not exist.

And finally, thanks to my wife, Dawn, for her encouragement and support.

Why Am I a Leader?

I'm not a Scout Leader for the easy hours, high pay, parents' gratitude, power or prestige.

I'm a Leader because I want the world for your son or daughter and mine.

A world they can share and help shape: a world of love and laughter where they can show compassion.

I want to help them learn to finish anything they start and do it well and to guide them to know their self-worth with a deeper understanding of themselves.

I want to help shape men and women who have strength of character and are sensitive to the needs of others.

I want them to be the best they can be, whether as career people or tradesmen, young adults who are the hearts of the family.

In giving of my time and myself I reap rewards far beyond what I give. I receive a better world for my children and future generations.

I'm a Scout Leader because I care.

Author Unknown

Prologue

On the way to work one morning, one of my carpool buddies asked me how old my son was. He grinned when I told him Randy was eight, and he invited us to join his Cub Scout pack. Even though there were no openings for new boys without additional Den Mothers, he would make room for Randy if I would take the job of Pinewood Derby Chairman. I had no idea what a Pinewood Derby was or what its chairman did, but I told him I would be happy to do the job. Little did I know what I was letting myself in for.

A few days later my son Randy, my wife, and I attended the Pack Recruitment Night and waited for Randy to be placed in a den. We had been seated in neighborhood groupings and as new dens were formed and boys were assigned to them, women stepped forward to become Den Mothers. Pretty soon, all the boys were in dens except Randy and eight other hopefuls in our group because, even though the women had been assured that being a Den Mother would only require an hour a week, no one had volunteered.

I knew there would be a place for the son of the Pinewood Derby Chairman, but what about the other eight boys? And then I got this great idea to embarrass one of the mothers into taking the job. I stood up and in a loud voice said, "Why not have the meetings in the evening with a Den Father?"

I really got their attention, but instead of volunteering they rose to their feet and in one voice said, "Great, you have the job."

I thought about this for a minute or two and then decided to decline the Pinewood Derby offer to become the first male Den Mother in the Northwest Suburban Council. That was in the spring of 1967, and if any of those mothers are reading this book, I would like them to know that I've forgiven them for not letting me become Pinewood Derby Chairman.

During the years that followed, I held many different positions in Scouting. Some were more fun than work and a few the other way around. Without any doubt, though, the jobs that allowed me to be directly involved with boys were the best, and those are the memories and stories that I will share with you in this book

Larry

Chapter 1.   Let's Get Started

Now that I was a Den Mother, I enrolled in the training course for new Cub Scout leaders. There were four two-hour sessions and everyone attended the first two, which focused on the overall Cub Scout program. The last two sessions were job-specific, so I went to the Den Mother classroom. The instructor kept trying to send me to the Webelos Den Leader or Cubmaster training rooms and really had trouble believing I was a Den Mother. It must have been my failure to be in uniform. He reluctantly allowed me to stay but he gave me strange looks all evening.

A few of the men in the first training sessions were not in uniform, so I didn't give much thought to my attire. However, all the women in the first Den Mother session wore yellow blouses and blue skirts or pants, so I felt I should do so, too. I bought a yellow shirt and a pair of blue pants (I didn't have the legs for a skirt), and my wife sewed on all the appropriate patches. I was certain that I would now blend in with the other Den Mothers at our last training class and gain the instructor's approval.

But instead of securing that approval, I was

asked to step outside and explain why I was disrupting the training session. It took me nearly 15 minutes to tell him how I had happened to become a Den Mother and to convince him that I was serious about learning what I had to do. He let me back in the session, but I don't think he really believed my story.

As soon as my training was complete, I started having den meetings with the boys. I wasn't sure I was doing everything correctly, but the boys all seemed to enjoy the activities, and so did I. In fact, after a few weeks I felt brave enough to plan a Saturday trip to the Museum of Science and Industry.

I recruited two other parents for this trip and I told the boys to wear their uniforms so we could locate them easily if they moved away from our little group. I wish I had known the museum was sponsoring Cub Scout Day and the halls would be filled with hundreds of identically dressed boys.

By the time Halloween rolled around, I was very comfortable with my role as Den Mother. Since everyone needed to be in costume for our pack meeting, I decided to go as Little Red Riding Hood. I bought a blond wig and my wife bought some red fabric and sewed a cloak for me. Just before we left for the pack meeting she went to work on my face with her make-up kit. I drew the line at having my eyebrows plucked, but I thought I looked pretty good, anyway. There were prizes for the best costumes and even though I didn't win, two guys asked me out and a third proposed marriage.

Chapter 2.   Fire Alarm

I felt more confident about my role as Den Mother with each passing month, and I started to look for activities that would augment the weekly den meetings we held at my house and the monthly pack meetings we attended at the grammar school that sponsored us. Holding the interest of nine eight-year old boys was quite a challenge.

There was a fire station a few blocks from my house, and the lieutenant told me that I could bring the boys by for a tour of the firehouse and a look into the job of the firefighter. He told me that he would sound the alarm bell and have one or two of his men put on their coats so the boys could experience a little bit of what it was like to be a firefighter. He also made certain that I knew where to have the boys stand when the alarm sounded.

When we arrived at the fire station, the boys were given a tour and then allowed to climb up a few steps on a ladder and slide down the fire pole, try on an actual helmet and sit in the fire truck. They were even allowed to sound the siren. And with Smokey, a Dalmatian who loved kids, giving them all his attention, the boys were in sheer ecstasy. I did have to say no, though, when they wanted to try the fire hoses.

Suddenly, the fire alarm sounded. I was expecting the demonstration we had been promised, but something about the firefighters' response to the bell told me that this was no mere performance; this was the real thing. I hustled the boys over to our designated spot near the wall to be out of everyone's way. They watched wide-eyed and barely breathing as the men slid down the pole, put on their fire fighting equipment and jumped onto two fire trucks, which roared out of the fire station with sirens at full volume.

After the boys thanked the firefighters remaining in the station, we headed back to my house for milk and cookies. I couldn't help overhearing their conversation as they tried to figure out how I had arranged to have a real fire alarm sound during our visit.

Chapter 3.   Who Will Be Den Mother?

One year after becoming Den Mother, I bought a larger house in Des Plaines, Illinois, and that meant my family and I would be moving away. I didn't want to leave without finding a replacement, but once again no one wanted the job. I met with the parents, first as a group and then individually, but with no luck. I knew I would have to do something drastic to keep the boys in the program. But what?

Finally I had an idea. I invited all the boys and their parents for a good-bye party at my house, and I emphasized that I wanted the boys to be in uniform. Everyone showed up and the party went very well; they even bought a gift for me. I'm sure they wouldn't have done that if they had known what I had in mind.

After the cake and ice cream had disappeared, I asked my wife to take all the boys into the other room while I talked with the parents. I tried one last time to get one of them to become Den Mother, but without any luck. I do have to admit, though, that some of their excuses were really creative. Especially the woman who was considering having another child and didn't want a long-term commitment. I think they were starting to suspect my little party was a ploy to get a new leader. But I was ready for them.

I asked the boys to come back into the room and then told them to take off their uniform shirts and to stand next to their parents.

"Okay, boys," I said, "You are all out of Cub Scouts and I would like you to ask your moms and dads why."

It took less than five minutes to get a Den Mother and two assistants. I met one of the moms a few months later at a shopping mall. "You weren't very nice at your party," she said.

"Is Joey still in Cub Scouts?" I asked.

"Of course," she answered. I just smiled at her and she thought for a few minutes before she started to leave. She took a few steps and then turned back and smiled. "Thanks" was all she said.

Chapter 4.   Amaquonsippi Trail

After moving to our new house and joining a new pack, I became an Assistant Cubmaster, and a year later was asked by the Pack Committee to serve as Cubmaster. I didn't have as much contact with the boys as I did when I was a Den Mother, but I think this gig was just setting me up for what was to come next. My son Randy and I joined a Boy Scout troop and I became the most inexperienced Assistant Scoutmaster in BSA history.

I immediately signed up for training, but our troop's scheduled Amaquonsippi campout and hike came before I had a chance to attend any of the training classes. We left early on a Saturday morning and arrived in Bradford, Illinois–a sleepy little town about 80 miles from Des Plaines–just in time to set up camp and have a quick lunch before starting our hike. The fact that the campground was right next to a very large pig farm added a little ambience to our dining experience.

If the weather is nice, the Amaquonsippi trail is quite enjoyable. It meanders through the woods and across farmers' fields for 16 miles, starting and ending at the campground. I had never hiked before, but if these 11-year-old kids could do it, I was sure I could, too. After all, I had my brand-new hiking boots and a poncho which the Scoutmaster, Carl Thomas, had reminded me to bring and which I was certain I wouldn't need. The sun was shining and I was finally getting used to the pig smell. It was great day for a hike.

I was assigned the job of walking at the end of the line and making certain that none of the boys got behind me. Easy enough, I thought, and away we went. The first hour was just as I had expected, and I did my job at the end of the line without any problems. And then the rain came. Not a nice gentle spring rain, but a torrential downpour. It wasn't too long before I could no longer see the front of our group, and this caused me great concern because I knew neither where I was going nor what I was supposed to be doing in addition to not letting any kids get behind me.

Did I mention that this was April and the farmers had just plowed the fields we were walking across? Rain and freshly turned dirt combine to form the mud equivalent of quicksand. As the rain eased up a little, I could see the head of our line and it was farther away than I wanted it to be. I wondered whether part of the training I was going to take covered not losing people. I tried to walk a little faster, but Marty Graves was right in front of me and I realized that he was part of the reason I was so far behind. This was also Marty's first campout and hike and I think he was the only person in our group who knew less than I did.

Marty was a very short boy, and his mother (who was both thrifty and optimistic that he would grow) had made a rather large hem at the bottom of his poncho and fastened it with masking tape. It didn't take very long for the water and mud to work the tape loose, causing the poncho to drag behind him and trip him every few steps.

Did I also mention that the farmers had separated their fields with barbed wire and we had to climb styles (two or three wooden steps up to the top of the fence and then down the other side) to get over them? Marty's poncho snagged on the barbed wire every time we tried to cross, and this was slowing us down even more.

"Marty," I said, "I need to cut off the bottom part of your poncho or we're going to be left behind."

"No, you can't do that," he answered. "My

mother will kill me if you do."

I gave him my most ferocious look and said, "You don't know that for sure, but just think about what I will do if you don't let me cut it."

He reluctantly agreed, and I cut 18 inches off the bottom of the poncho. Our pace was a little better after that, and I thought we were even gaining ground.

The trail finally left the fields and went alongside a bluff that overlooked the river, so we made a little better time and we were able to catch up with the rest of the troop. It helped that they had stopped to rest.

Mr. Thomas came over to me and explained that the trail now went straight up a 50- or 60-foot hill. There was a steel cable that stretched from our trail to the top of the hill. You were supposed to hold onto it and pull yourself up. I guess this worked very well when it was dry, but in the rain and mud that cable was very slick.

"Your job," he said to me, "is to stay here at the bottom of the hill and catch any of the boys if they slip and fall. You have to catch them before they fall into the river. I'm going to go up first so I can give the boys a hand as they come up and then you climb up after all the boys have made it."

I was pretty pleased that he had given me this responsibility until I realized that there would be no one to catch me if I fell. Talk about being expendable.

I actually caught three boys sliding down the hill and then, much to my amazement, I made it up to the top. The rain had slowed to a light mist–the kind that gets into your bones and chills you so that you never can get warm. By this time, my feet were aching and I was sure I had blisters, but I didn't want to look because I didn't have the slightest idea what I should do if I did see any. We had been hiking for hours and I was sure that we would see our camp at any moment. I kept sniffing the air, hoping to get a whiff of those wonderful pigs.

I couldn't believe my ears when I heard one of the older boys yell, "Here is the cable bridge; we're half way."

I don't know who invented cable bridges, because there has to be a better way to cross a river. There were two steel cables, about five feet apart, spanning the black, rushing water. You stood on the lower one, held onto the upper one, and sidestepped across the river. And once again

I had to make sure all the boys, especially the shorter ones, had a good grip so they could safely make the trip.

When it was finally my turn, I thought I was doing quite well until I heard one of the boys yell, "Don't worry if you fall, Mr. B. I have my lifesaving merit badge." Thankfully, I didn't need to be rescued on this bridge or the three other ones we also had to cross.

I'm not sure how I managed to finish the hike, because every muscle in my body was screaming and my feet were so sore that I just barely limped along. It was dark when we finally returned to camp, and now that the hike was over the rain also came to an end. I was afraid that if I sat down I would never get up again, so I leaned against a tree, trying to get the energy to go to bed. I hoped Mr. Thomas wouldn't ask me to see that every boy got into his tent.

Pretty soon, one of the boys came up to me and handed me something called hamburger stew in foil and told me that this was my dinner. I was so hungry that I wolfed it right down. It didn't bother me a bit that everything was a little cold and the meat was a little gushy and the veggies were a little crunchy. It was probably a special kind of Boy Scout dinner that I would learn about later.

The next morning I overheard one of the boys telling another one that Mr. B must have been really hungry because he ate his dinner without cooking it.

I had just completed my first 16-mile hike and eaten my first camp dinner and now I was about to spend my first night in a tent. I limped over to the tent, unrolled my brand-new $29 supermarket sleeping bag and got undressed. As soon as I crawled into the sleeping bag I knew something was wrong. There were rocks of all sizes and shapes under the tent and I could feel every one of them. It took me half an hour to move them enough so I could be comfortable and I made a mental note to be sure to buy an air mattress if I ever did this again.

Just as I was about to doze off, I got a gentle reminder from my bladder that I had neglected one more thing. This meant getting out of my sleeping bag, getting dressed and looking for a bathroom (which turned out to be a large tree at a discreet distance from the campsite). Once that was taken care of, I went back to bed, rearranged my rocks and managed to fall asleep.

I felt pretty good in the morning until I tried to get out of the sleeping bag and found that I couldn't move. It took me nearly an hour to get up and put on some clothes. I managed to get out of the tent, but every step was a new experience in pain. I couldn't believe that I had done this of my own free will and that I would be expected to do it again. There had to be another, less painful, job in Scouting, and as soon as I could walk I was going to find it.

Just then the Senior Patrol Leader came up to me with a steaming cup of coffee. He handed it to me and said,

"You did pretty well for your first time, Mr. B, and next time will be better."

Maybe this Assistant Scoutmaster stuff wasn't so bad, after all.

15

Chapter 5.   The Great Snipe Hunt

After two months in the troop, I got to know the boys and even began looking forward to our Spring Camp-O-Ree. Little did I know what awaited me.

We arrived at the camping area Friday evening, and the boys set up camp in record time so we could all enjoy our evening campfire. They seemed particularly secretive and kept laughing and looking at me as I sat and enjoyed a cup of coffee. On our last campout they had me turning in circles, waving my arms and chanting "Owa-tagu-siam" as I tried to appease the rain spirits and keep them away for another day (you can try this yourself if you would like to get the full effect). I wondered what they had up their collective sleeves this time.

Saturday was devoted to patrol competition and I enjoyed watching the Scouts use the skills they had mastered. I even was asked to judge some of the events, and I felt as though I was really a part of the troop. When the day's events were over, we returned to our campsite for dinner.

In our troop, each patrol invited a different adult to eat each meal with them and, since our

Scouts were pretty good cooks, I eagerly looked forward to dinner. I noticed that the boys were still whispering and looking over at me just as they had done on Friday evening, but I was hungry and the stew smelled great, so I just put any concerns out of my mind.

Once dinner was over and our dishes had been cleaned up, the boys went to our Scoutmaster and asked to go on a scavenger hunt. He readily agreed and told them that they should put their teams together while he made up lists of items. In a few minutes the Senior Patrol Leader came over to where I was sitting with the other Assistant Scoutmasters and asked whether we would like to join them—one adult with each team. The other three jumped right up and agreed, so, of course, I followed their lead and did the same.

Our team seemed to have a lot of older boys, but that fact slipped right past me as we all looked over the list of things we needed to find. There were about 15 items, and along with green string, yellow buttons and three-pronged forks were several things I had never heard of. I had no idea what a skyhook or a smoke bender looked like or whether we could even carry thirty feet of shoreline. And what, in heaven's name, was a snipe?

Some of these strange items were not only in great demand, but also in very short supply. It appeared that every Scoutmaster we questioned had just lent his last one to some other troop at the opposite end of the camp. After two hours of fruitless search we returned to our camp and I was sure that we hadn't done very well in the scavenger hunt. And I still had no idea what a snipe was.

I kept looking at the other teams as they came back into camp to see whether they had been able to find all their items, but they weren't about to divulge anything to me and I didn't really want to be too obvious. So I went looking for my son, Randy, and asked him how his team had done, but he wasn't going to give me any more information than the other kids. When I couldn't hold back any more, I just came right out and asked him if he knew what a snipe was and whether he had found his. All I received for an answer was that we would be going on a snipe hunt to catch them. Beyond that, his lips were sealed.

A few minutes later, one of the boys on my team came over to me and asked whether I was ready to go on the snipe hunt to get the last item on our list. I said that I was and then he asked whether I knew what a snipe was and how to capture one.

While I was trying to think of a way to tell the truth without appearing too dumb, he said, "Here's how we do it in our troop." He then proceeded to explain that the team would go into the woods and chase the little creature towards me. When it came near me, I was to shine my flashlight into its eyes, causing it to freeze in its tracks. Then I was to get it into a burlap sack and bring it back to camp. I looked around and saw that everyone else was getting ready for this great adventure, so I told him okay, and off we went.

We walked into the woods for about twenty minutes and then the boys told me to wait with my flashlight and sack until the snipe came toward me. And off they went. I heard them talking and laughing for a few minutes, and then there was nothing. Just the night sounds of the woods. They had cautioned me to be very quiet but after about ten minutes I decided to call out because there were no snipes in sight and I wanted to be sure they were chasing it towards me. There was no answer, and I began to be a little concerned that they might be lost.

Another ten minutes passed, and I decided to head back to camp without my snipe. I was sure I would be the only one who didn't get one. We had taken a very circuitous route into the woods, and it took me nearly an hour to find my way back to our camp. The laughing boys and grinning adults who greeted me told the whole story.

When I first joined the troop, I had noticed that the adults wore the same gold neckerchiefs as the boys. I had asked our Scoutmaster where I could buy one and he answered that I couldn't and then changed the subject. I had thought this was rather strange, but so was a lot of the other stuff I was encountering, so I didn't give it any more thought. Sunday morning, as we prepared to pack up our equipment, the Senior Patrol Leader called the whole troop together and then asked me to come forward.

He handed me a small wrapped package, and when I looked at him, he told me to please open it. Inside the package were a beautiful gold neckerchief and a note that read, "Welcome to our troop."

I still get warm fuzzies when I think about it.

Chapter 6.   The Hangman's Noose

After I took Scoutmaster training and spent a few months in the troop, I began to feel much more comfortable with the Scouting program and I really regretted the fact that I had not been a Scout as a boy.

On one of our monthly campouts, David Barish, one of our younger Scouts, discovered the hangman's noose. He had been working with a rope for quite some time and I was pleased to see him practicing his knots so diligently until our Scoutmaster, Mr. Thomas, and I went over to compliment him and saw what he was making.

"That's a very nice noose, Dave," said Mr. Thomas. "Now take it apart and work on something else."

David took the noose apart, but a short time later he refashioned it and this time he was wearing it around his neck.

Mr. Thomas was a little more adamant when he stopped him this time, but an hour or so later, there it was again, and this time the excess rope was dragging on the ground. We could see a disaster just waiting to happen. Mr. Thomas took the rope and told David, in no uncertain terms, that he was not to touch it again. He seemed to get the message because we didn't see the noose again for the rest of the day.

Sunday morning, however, was another story; there was the noose around David's neck. Mr. Thomas didn't say a word this time. Instead, he got one of our largest soup pots, fastened a yoke for it, filled it with rocks and hung this around David's neck. That seemed to solve the problem because David was so busy trying to hold up the pot, he didn't have the time to make another noose.

Two hours later it was time to leave for home and it just so happened that David's father was one of the drivers who had volunteered to pick us up. He took one look at his son and stormed over to Mr. Thomas for an explanation. Five minutes later he walked away from us, picked up a large rock and put it into David's pot. I didn't hear what he said to his son as he added his rock to the load, but I'm sure it was not very sympathetic.

Chapter 7.   The Lincoln Trail

By the time I had spent a year in the troop I had become a pretty good camper and hiker. I even learned to be sure to break in new hiking boots before going on a hike and to clear away rocks before setting up my tent. So when we made plans to camp in New Salem, Illinois, and hike the 20-mile Lincoln Trail, I was sure I was ready.

The Scouts had to be at least first class in rank in order to hike the trail. They also were required to read a book about Abraham Lincoln, write a book report and submit it to the local BSA Council in order to receive the trail patch. Since we were a pretty young troop, there were only three boys who were going to do the hike: Jerry Barnes, Joe Carter and my son, Randy. An adult had to accompany the boys, and I was surprised and pleased when Mr. Thomas asked me to go.

Saturday's temperature was supposed to be in the high 90s, so I woke the boys a little early, hoping we could get most of the hike completed in the cooler part of the morning. We put our lunches into a small daypack, which the boys were to take turns carrying, filled our canteens, and away we went. It was 7:30 in the morning and Mr. Thomas was going to meet us in Springfield at 4:00 in the afternoon. With the expected heat, 8-1/2 hours would let us go at a slightly slower pace than usual.

I hate to be critical of hiking trails, but this one was terrible. The first three miles were on a marked trail through the woods, but the balance was on blacktop highway. We made great time during the morning (there was absolutely nothing along the way to look at), and we stopped for lunch around noon. There was a small convenience store nearby, and we were able to buy some munchies and refill our canteens. I figured we had walked about twelve miles.

The heat got to all of us after lunch, and by 2:00 I was really miserable and the boys began getting ahead of me. They devised a very simple hike plan. They would walk until they had almost lost sight of me and then find a shade tree where they would sit and rest. Just as I caught up to them they would get back on their feet and, letting me know how nice it was of them to wait for me, take off again.

By this time, I was doing my best James Whitmore WWII movie imitation. That's the one where his feet are wrapped in rags (the reasons alternate between burns, frostbite and blisters), and he shuffles along the road because he can't march any more. My little performance worked because the boys came back and decided to walk the last mile or so with me.

The hike ended at City Hall, where I signed the boys' hike cards and put them under the door. All that was left to do was to wait for Mr. Thomas to show up and take us back to camp. He did. And right on time, too.

Nothing had ever looked as good as that ice-cold soda or felt as good as taking those boots off and giving my feet a rest. I settled back to relax and looked for Randy, Jerry and Joe to find out whether they had experienced any ill effects from the heat. It took me a few minutes to locate them because they were in an open field playing softball with the rest of our troop. It's nice to be young.

The boys had given me their book reports and I had sent them to the Council office, along with their orders for trail medals and patches. I had also included the money for a patch of my own. Two weeks later I received the items for the boys, but my money had been returned with a note saying that I had not turned in the book report so I could not buy a patch. I tried again, carefully explaining that I was an adult and shouldn't be held to the same requirements as a Scout, but once again it was returned to me. If I wanted a patch, I'd have to do the Abraham Lincoln book report. So I did.

Chapter 8.   Change Your Underwear

Summer camp was something that the boys always looked forward to and, in my first summer with the troop, so did I. Mr. Thomas and I were taking our entire troop to Camp Namekogen in northern Wisconsin, so we chartered a bus for the 400-mile trip. We loaded up in the church parking lot, and as the parents all said good-bye I overheard David Barish's mother remind him to change his underwear every day. That seemed like a pretty normal thing for a mother to tell an adolescent boy, so I didn't give it another thought.

A few days after arriving at Namekogen, David asked me for permission to call home. He said that he had run out of money and wanted his parents to send him some. He made his call but came away from the phone booth mumbling under his breath. I asked him whether everything was okay and he said that his mother was acting strangely.

"I don't have any money," he said, "and all she can talk about is changing my underwear."

I knew David's mother very well, since we were classmates in high school, and she certainly wasn't going to let him go to camp without money. But since David's financial situation wasn't one of my priority items, I gave him two dollars and forgot about it.

Two days later, David called home again. "I still haven't gotten any money and now I owe almost everybody," he complained. His call home produced exactly the same result as the first, with David walking around and grumbling about his lack of money and his mother's preoccupation with his underwear.

Maybe I should have tried harder to help him, but since the only things the boys could buy at the camp store were candy bars, soda pop and ice cream, I just let it go. By the time we were ready to leave Namekogen and head for home, David had called his mother five times but had never received any money. I thought about this and decided I'd talk to her when we got home. It was a long ride and David was really working himself into a frazzle.

The bus had barely stopped when David was off and looking for his mother. When he found her, his two weeks of frustration all came tumbling out. "I didn't have any money and I couldn't buy anything and I owe money to all the other kids and I even owe Mr. T and Mr. B money and all you ever wanted to talk about was underwear."

"Dave," she answered, "did you ever change your underwear at camp?"

I could see the "here she goes again with the underwear" look start to cross his face but 0before he could answer, she took him by the arm and led him over to the pile of backpacks and duffel bags that had been unloaded from the bus.

I watched as she found David's bag and pulled it to the side. Without saying a word she opened it, exposing several sets of neatly folded underwear. She lifted the first pair of undershorts and stepped back. David's eyes went wide as he saw the three ten-dollar bills tucked inside.

Chapter 9.   Mammoth Cave

While we were still at Namekogen, I had asked Randy whether he would like his patrol to go on a special camping trip. He thought that was a great idea and got the rest of his patrol members together to hear what I had to say.

"If you complete all the requirements you need to advance a rank, I'll take you anywhere you want to go, up to 400 miles," I said. "And to make it even better, I'll do all the cooking and cleanup."

Randy, Dan, Jason, Joe, Frank and Tim really liked this idea and they all accepted my challenge. I enjoyed watching them because they were working together and it was great seeing the older boys helping the younger ones. With three days left at camp, they all came up to me with their record books. Except for active service, they had all completed the rank requirements and had decided that they wanted to go to Mammoth Cave in Kentucky. I also assured them that they would not have to work on any advancement while we were away; this would be a fun trip.

Once we got home, I called Ben Roberts (the father of one of the boys in the patrol), who had a van that would hold all of us, and he agreed to go along. The boys slept on my living room floor Wednesday night so we could leave at 4:00 AM on Thursday. They also slept through most of the drive and we arrived at the Mammoth Cave campground in mid-afternoon.

After we had set up our camp, the boys went exploring, and Mr. Roberts and I checked out the things we could do after going through the main cave. I found a map of hiking trails, and it occurred to me this would be the perfect opportunity for the boys to begin working on the hiking merit badge requirements. All I needed was a way to convince them that it was their idea.

On Friday morning, we went through Mammoth Cave, and since it was still early in the morning, I suggested that we pack a lunch and walk to the river, where we could take a boat ride. We walked along one of the trails that twisted just enough to make it a ten-mile trip. With the boat trip foremost on their minds they were eager to get started and didn't pay too much attention to the length of the hike. In fact, they never even noticed that the direct route back to camp was a little over three miles.

I had offered to do all the cooking and

cleanup, but I had no intention of spending all my time doing it. My menu selections were based on ease of preparation and cleanup. I had individual packages of cold cereal for the mornings, cold cut sandwiches for lunch and hamburgers or steaks for dinner, along with salad and cooked veggies served on paper plates with plastic knives and forks, so I had only ten minutes of cleanup a day. The boys never watched to see how much time I was spending on kitchen duty because they were just happy that I was doing it at all.

The next morning, the boys found a smaller cave that they wanted to visit, and I found an alternate trail that we could take to get there that just happened to be 10 miles long. What a coincidence! Later that afternoon, when we were back in camp, I managed to leave a brochure for the "Flags of the Nations" hiking trail on our table. The trail patches for this hike were beautiful, and it didn't take long before the boys were admiring them. I really made them work to convince me that, since it wasn't too far out of the way, we could stop there on the way home.

We got to the trail late Sunday morning and hiked the 20 miles in approximately 7 hours, since it wasn't very difficult. The boys and I bought all kinds of patches and then settled in for the ride home. An hour or so into the trip I asked the boys whether any of them knew the requirements for the hiking merit badge. It took a little time but they finally came up with the answer: five 10 milers and a 20, but they still didn't show much enthusiasm for completing it.

"Remember the walk we took on Friday?" I asked. "That was your first 10, and the walk on Saturday was the second."

"And this was the 20," hollered one of the boys. "We only have three more to do."

It wasn't too long before they had worked out a plan to do 10-mile hikes on each of the next two Saturdays and then the last one on our upcoming campout. After completing the written work they would then have the badges for our next Court of Honor, only six weeks away.

It was Mr. Roberts' turn to drive, so I closed my eyes and settled back in the seat. Maybe they wouldn't notice the smile that kept crossing my face.

Chapter 10.   Gotcha!

Our troop held a Court of Honor every three months, and it was always a lively, gratifying event. In addition to the awards, there were skits by the boys and refreshments afterwards. The boys must have met secretly and conspired to have some fun at the leaders' expense because we kept hearing little things like "They're too old to put on a skit," "It probably wouldn't be very funny," and "They're chicken." That last one did it.

Mr. Thomas, Mr. Carter (our other Assistant Scoutmaster) and I decided that we would do a world-class skit and poke some fun at the boys. We were going to impersonate inexperienced Scouts preparing for a winter campout. Harold Allen, our Committee Chairman, was going to play the role of Scoutmaster, but we weren't even going to tell him what we had in mind.

Mr. Allen had a unique personality. He could completely lose control and fly into a rage one minute and then put his arm around your shoulders and invite you for coffee the next. There will be much more about him later, but I've told you enough for now.

The Court of Honor went very well, and the boys all received the awards they had earned and the recognition they deserved. They did their skits, and finally it was time for ours.

We reminded Mr. Allen that he was playing the part of Scoutmaster, and we went into the outer hall to get ready.

Mr. Thomas went first. He had no coat, all his gear was in a supermarket plastic bag, and he was dragging his sleeping bag. Mr. Allen took one look and then let him know how unprepared he was and what a disgrace he was to our troop, the BSA, and humanity in general.

Mr. Carter entered next, pulling his backpack, which had every item of clothing hanging out of the pockets. His mess kit was tied on and clanked at every step. Mr. Allen went after him, too, and finally sent him home to repack his equipment.

When I came in wearing short pants and sneakers, he really lost control. He forgot that this was a skit and actually believed that we were boys reporting for a winter overnighter. The last straw was when I told him that my mother didn't have any money and asked whether he would pay my expenses for the weekend. It wasn't until the laughter and applause drowned out all the other sounds that he realized it was all in good fun.

As the Senior Patrol Leader prepared to end the evening's program, he acknowledged the parents and boys who had helped and then ended with "Thanks to Mr. Thomas, Mr. Bernstein, Mr. Carter and Mr. Allen for a cool skit."

That's a boy's equivalent of a standing ovation.

Chapter 11.   First Aid Meet

The Scouts always looked forward to our annual District First Aid competition and spent a lot of time practicing for them. Each patrol had to supply its own "victims" and, since some of the problems were quite complex, usually invited youngsters in the audience to help out. My daughter, Michelle, and my younger son, Scott, were always eager volunteers, and I was happy to see them get involved.

I usually acted as a patrol judge during this competition and didn't pay particular attention to Michelle and Scott. They would always be lying on blankets with boys bandaging various parts of their anatomy. During one complicated problem, Scott must have acted up, because the boys bandaged him from head to toe, told him he was a mummy and left him in a corner for twenty minutes.

One year I was the chairman of the meet and could not serve as a judge. This gave me a chance to walk around and check on how my boys were doing. In previous years they had accepted Michelle as a victim because they had to have one and she was available. But now she was growing up, and so were the boys. This time, I discovered they were arguing over which boys would get to do CPR and mouth-to-mouth resuscitation. That was the last time I let her participate, and she still hasn't forgiven me.

Chapter 12.   A Boy Is Missing

For quite a while, the older boys in our troop had been asking to go on a Philmont Scout Ranch trek, and the Troop Committee decided that this was the year to do it. Our Scoutmaster, Mr. Thomas, would take the older boys to Philmont and I would take the seventeen younger boys to Camp Napowan for two weeks. My employer was very supportive of my Scouting activities, so I could be there for the entire two weeks and assorted fathers would come to help out for as many days as they could manage.

I liked to see the Scouts earn merit badges at summer camp, so our routine was pretty simple. The boys worked on water merit badges in the morning and other badges of their choice after lunch, until 4:00 or so. For the rest of the day they had free time, unless we had some type of planned activity, such as a hike. One day, the boys asked me whether we could take an all-day canoe trip. This would be a nice break from the daily camp routine, so I told our Senior Patrol Leader to pick the day and get us signed up.

On the day of our trip, there were two fathers at camp with us, and they also wanted to go canoeing. We rode one of the camp buses to the river, and as we were about to get started, I took a final count: there were seventeen boys, two dads, two coolers with our lunches, and me. I was going to have one of the adults in the first canoe, I would be somewhere in the middle of the group, and the third adult, who just happened to be an experienced canoeist, would bring up the rear.

There had been quite a bit of rain just before our trip, and the water was a little higher and faster and a lot blacker than normal. There were little mini-whitecaps lapping at the shore. But I had been told that the river was safe and we should go ahead with the trip as planned. I reminded the dad who would be in the last canoe that he was not to let any canoe get behind him (boy, did that sound familiar).

The trip went very well for the first two or three hours. The faster water kept the paddling to a minimum and the boys were having a great time. I lost sight of the canoes ahead of me as they made a sharp left turn, but I didn't think anything of it until our canoe made the same turn. There, spanning almost the entire river, was a fallen tree, and as each canoe made the turn it immediately hit the tree and flipped over.

As my head came up out of the water, I made sure that the boy who had been riding with me was safe and holding onto our canoe, and then I looked around. There were overturned canoes and boys hanging onto them for as far as I could see. From the laughter and splashing that was going on, I got the feeling that the boys were safe and having great fun, so I took another look at my own situation.

Timmy and I were holding on to our canoe but couldn't touch bottom and it was impossible to lift the canoe high enough to empty the water and turn it upright. So we did the next best thing. We climbed into the canoe and started paddling with our hands. Aluminum canoes are designed so that they won't sink, but when filled with water and with two people in them, they float under the water instead of on the surface.

Just in case this picture isn't clear, let me describe it a little better. A boy submerged up to his chin and a man submerged up to his armpits are using their hands to paddle down the river. If you looked under the water, you would see both of them kneeling in a canoe that was floating 15 inches below the surface. Paddles, coolers, canoes and even a boy or two floated past but were just out of reach.

The river finally widened enough to slow the current and we were able to get to shore, where the other boys were waiting. No one was hurt, and the canoes, paddles and even our slightly soggy lunches had all been recovered. The boys who had been behind me began coming out of the water and then the last canoe showed up. It was the only one that had not swamped.

I took a quick count and came up with sixteen boys, so I counted again. I still got sixteen.

"Nobody move," I told the boys and started a very careful and deliberate count. Again the total was sixteen. I could feel the panic starting as I lined up the boys to see which one was missing. A massive feeling of dread washed over me as I realized that I had lost a boy I was responsible for.

"It's Billy!" one of the boys yelled. "Billy's not here."

Just then, Ed Dunne, the dad who had been in our last canoe, came over to me.

"I had a problem when we were getting into the canoes," he said. "Billy got scared and started crying and said he was afraid to go. The bus driver told me he would take him back to camp and have another Scoutmaster watch him until we returned. I didn't know what else to do, so I let him go. Was that the right thing to do?"

I've never had much of an urge to kiss another man, but in this case I believe I could have made an exception.

Chapter 13.   Trap Door

One of the friends I made through the Scouting program was Art Schwartz, an Assistant Scoutmaster in a troop in a neighboring community. He was also an instructor at Indiana University and an expert in spelunking and rappelling. He lived in Bloomington, Indiana, and usually restricted his Scouting duties to weekends and school vacations. He had offered to take our troop spelunking a number of times, and we finally decided to take him up on it.

The area surrounding Bloomington was dotted with hundreds of undeveloped caves, both large and small. These caves had no lights and no pathways and were not open to general sightseers. There were only a few simple rules. You had to sign in at the entrance to the cave, listing all names and when you expected to exit. You could never go in alone and you had to wear a hard hat. Art provided us with the hard hats and headlamps.

Our first cave was called "Trap Door" because you entered the cave through a hole in the ground that was covered with a garbage can lid. You went into the cave feet first and then slithered through three sharp S bends to reach the bottom of this shaft. When we were all together, Art led the way. I was in the middle (a promotion, I believe), and Mr. Thomas, our Scoutmaster, was at the end. We would alternate walking and crawling, with our goal "an awesome sight" about one mile ahead.

We were progressing nicely until we reached our first obstacle. There was a small opening in the rock that we had to crawl through. Art and the boys in front of me had already made their way through by the time I reached it.

"I'll never fit," I yelled through the hole.

"Sure you will," came the reply. "I'm bigger than you and I've made it through without any trouble."

I believed him because I knew that Scouters always tell the truth. And with encouraging words from the boys in back of me ("Hurry up, Mr. B, we don't want to be left behind"), I slowly started sliding through the opening.

About halfway through, I got stuck. And I mean seriously stuck. I couldn't go forward and I couldn't go back. I knew there were boys in front of me and behind me, so at least I wouldn't be left alone until I lost enough weight to be able to back out. I surely didn't want to go forward, because then I'd have to go through that thing again on the way back. Just in case I forgot to mention it, you go into a cave and explore it. When you are ready to leave, you turn around and retrace your steps.

By this time I was pretty scared and, of course, that made me hyperventilate and get wedged even tighter. Suddenly the image of Winnie the Pooh getting stuck in the entrance to Rabbit's home popped into my mind. It took him three or four days to get skinny enough to get "unstuck." That was not an encouraging thought.

"Don't panic," Art told me.

"You're too late," I responded. "I've already panicked. What comes next?"

"The top of the opening is sloped. Take three deep breaths and slide as far as you can to the left," he answered.

It's not easy taking deep breaths when you are doing your best cork-in-a-bottle imitation, but I tried. I was able to move just a bit, so I continued with the breaths and sliding and I finally managed to wiggle my way through the opening.

I looked for the boys and Mr. Thomas, who had been behind me, but there they all were, right in front of me. I can only imagine how I must have looked when they told me there was a way around the hole without going through it.

"I always walk around it," Art told me. "I figured if you could make it, I'd give it a try the next time I'm here."

The boys thought this was a riot, but I waited until I was safely out of the cave before I agreed with them.

Chapter 14.   I've Been Poisoned!

Every once in a while, the leaders would give the boys a break on a campout and cook a dinner for them. We each did a different part of the meal, and my responsibility was the main dish. My wife was a very good cook, and I got her secret recipe for sloppy joes. Well, the recipe wasn't exactly secret, but it did contain one secret ingredient, which I had promised not to disclose.

The meal was a huge success and the boys kept coming back for more salad, sloppy joes on fresh baked bread, veggies and cobbler. There was plenty of food and we all probably ate a bit more than we should have. My sloppy joes were particularly in demand and, when the boys wanted to know what made it taste so good, I would only tell them that it was my secret ingredient. They kept asking what it was, but I held firm and didn't say a word. At least not until my son Randy came over and, claiming special offspring privilege, asked again for the ingredient that made the taste so special. I finally gave in and told him that it was grape jelly.

His response was a very loud "*Yuck,* nobody puts that in sloppy joes," and he left to go about his business.

Two hours later the boys were all in their tents and I was getting ready to go to bed. I looked up and there was Randy, moaning and groaning.

"I'm sick, Dad," he said, "and Frank is throwing up in his sleeping bag. Your grape jelly poisoned us."

I felt really bad until I remembered that Randy had made several return trips to refill his plate. "Just how many sloppy joes did you eat tonight?" I asked him.

"Only six," he answered.

My sympathy for his discomfort disappeared very quickly, and when I checked on Frank, I found that he had brought a one-pound bag of potato chips along with him and had eaten the entire bag by himself.

My sloppy joes were exonerated.

Chapter 15.   Polar Bear Award

One of the lesser-known awards that Scouts can earn is the Polar Bear Award. There is only one requirement, and that is to spend one night in a tent during each of the five winter months of November, December, January, February and March. Some of the boys had read about this award in *Boys' Life* magazine and decided that they wanted to go for it.

Our Senior Patrol Leader had made the suggestion at our monthly Patrol Leaders' meeting, and Mr. Thomas, our Scoutmaster, thought it was a great idea except for one small detail: He didn't like to camp in cold weather. So he passed the buck to me. The entire troop would schedule its regular (weather permitting) campouts, but if it was too cold for the whole troop to go, I was to camp with the Polar Bear hopefuls. I must have forgotten to tell him I wasn't crazy about the idea of spending the night in a tent in freezing cold weather, either.

Winter started out very mild, and our November-through-February campouts were pretty routine. The thirteen Scouts who made all four outings were still eligible to try for the Polar

Bear Award. Mild weather was also predicted for all of March, and I was sure we had smooth camping ahead. Mr. Thomas was going to be out of town, so Sam Carter, Jack Rose (our two other Assistant Scoutmasters), and I would be going with the boys.

The troop planned a trip to Starved Rock State Park for our March campout and we had a number of hikes scheduled for the weekend. We had camped at this park before and the boys were looking forward to exploring the many canyons we would pass as we hiked.

We arrived at our campsite early Friday evening and, after setting up our tents and having dinner, everyone enjoyed hot chocolate and ghost stories around the glowing embers of our dying campfire. When I awoke on Saturday morning, it was quite chilly and I was eager to get a pot of coffee ready. As I unzipped my tent and stepped out, I certainly wasn't prepared for the 6-8 inches of snow that had fallen during the night. And from what I could see, it didn't look as if it would stop anytime in the near future.

We decided not to go hiking, but the boys were having so much fun in the snow, we didn't get any complaints. By early afternoon, another

4-5 inches of snow had fallen and Mr. Carter, Mr. Rose, and I started to discuss whether we should stay Saturday night or pack up and head for home. We never had to make that decision because the park ranger showed up at our campsite on his snowmobile (I was going to say "dogsled", but I didn't think you would believe me) and informed us that all roads had been closed and that we had better plan on staying through the night. We had brought enough food for the entire weekend, so there was no danger of cannibalism and, with the boys having such a great time, we didn't see any problem in staying.

The snowfall slowed a bit during the day but still showed no signs of stopping, and I was getting concerned about what Sunday morning would bring. A second visit from the ranger did little to make me feel better: He reported that the extended weather forecast was for continued snow, with temperatures dropping sharply on Sunday. And the roads were still closed.

By Saturday evening the snow had started to let up, and by the time we finished our dinner and campfire it had stopped completely. I could feel it getting colder but I was sure that we would be able to leave for home in the morning.

The snow started falling again during the night and the temperature kept dropping. When I awoke Sunday morning, the thermometer I wore on my jacket registered -15°, and even though the snow had stopped we had another 4-5 inches on the ground.

A third visit from the park ranger informing us that all roads were still closed didn't make any of the adults feel better, but the boys thought getting snowed in for another day or two and missing school was going to be quite an adventure. The ranger did offer to take one of the adults back to his house so that he could call the boys' parents (and our wives) and let them know that we probably would not be home on Sunday as planned. Mr. Carter went with the ranger and on the way back he even managed to stop at a local grocery store and replenish our food supply.

There were snow flurries all day Sunday, but our greatest concern was the dropping temperature. By dinnertime my thermometer read -20° and it wasn't much warmer inside our tents. As the boys got colder, their enthusiasm for this great adventure began to wane. Mr. Carter, Mr. Rose, and I decided that one of us would keep the campfire going through the night so that the boys could come out of their tents and warm up if they got too cold. We also found a few extra blankets in one of our vans that we passed out to them. By midnight the temperature had dropped to -22° and it seemed the night would never end.

It was barely dawn when the ranger showed up again, telling us to get ready to leave as soon as we could. The roads had been opened during the night, but a new storm front–with more snow–was approaching rapidly. He didn't have to tell us twice. We abandoned camp.

Once we reached the interstate highway and were on our way home, the boys' enthusiasm returned. They kept asking whether they had now earned their Polar Bear Awards and, when I assured them that they had, they decided to go for another one the following year.

That gave me about seven months to find some extra-heavy-duty thermal underwear and a warmer sleeping bag.

Chapter 16.　Proud to Be a Fox

After nearly two years in the troop I had an opportunity to take Wood Badge training, and I jumped at the chance. The course was still being taught in the one-week format (instead of the current three weekends), and I was really looking forward to it. I attended all the pre-training meetings and decided to buy a new uniform and sew on the appropriate patches, since there was no way I was going to remove all the patches from my existing shirt.

I also learned that BSA believes that if you have a large waist you also must have long legs, because the legs on my short uniform pants had been at least three inches below my knees. Luckily, I had tried them on before going to camp and my wife had shortened them for me.

There were 40-50 of us gathered at the Camp Napowan dining hall, eager and ready to begin our training. We were put into patrols and given compass directions to our various campsites. I had my compass handy, so my patrol members put on their backpacks and followed my lead. Right into the swamp.

I sheepishly admitted that I must have made

a small error and we went back to the starting point to try again with someone else leading the way. Everyone was certain that with a new navigator we would be at our campsite in a few minutes. We were now 15 minutes behind the other patrols, and on the first day of Wood Badge training 15 minutes is an eternity. We started out again, and in a few minutes, there we were. In the swamp.

Back to the starting point we went, and this time we took off our backpacks so we could really get serious because now we were a half hour behind. We made our third try a group effort, with every heading checked and double-checked before we moved even one step. We were determined to get it right. This time it took us twice as long to reach the swamp.

Wood Badge training, especially during the first few days, is based on the principle of *guided discovery.* This simply means that every question is answered with another question, which is supposed to lead you to discover the answer for yourself. This is a very effective method of teaching, except when it's your first day and directions to your campsite keep leading you into a swamp.

We finally found our Senior Patrol Leader and explained our dilemma. He was not especially sympathetic, but he did ask us why we were starting from the dining hall. "Because that's where it says to start," we told him.

"Really?" he answered. "Everyone else started from the flagpole."

We tried once more, using the flagpole as our starting point, and in just a few minutes we were at a real campsite. The platform bases were there but we had to set up our tents, sew patches on our shirts, cook dinner and complete the assignment we would need for our first morning class. Having spent an hour or so exploring the swamp didn't help, and we didn't get to bed until 3:00 in the morning.

Wood Badge training is a very intensive program. In addition to the formal presentations, there are all kinds of little things that you have to figure out for yourself. For example, we had points deducted every morning at inspection until we realized that one of our patrol members had turned up his pants (the large waist-long leg syndrome). There was no break in the intensity for the first four days, and we never got to bed before 2 AM. In fact, that was the only time we had the opportunity to take showers.

Our routine during these first days never varied. Wake up at 5:00 AM, breakfast at 6:00 and line up in formation at the flagpole at 7:00 for flag-raising and inspection. We were observed and graded on everything we did, because the best patrol would be recognized at the end of the week. And when I say "observed," I'm not joking. We were a little late one morning and had a cold breakfast instead of a cooked one. Demerits. One patrol member was too tired to shower. Demerits. We never were able to figure out how the staff managed to learn our secrets. And they weren't talking.

It doesn't matter whether you are at Camp Napowan for one day or twenty days. Inevitably you will get rained on. Our storm came on our third day, and it was a real downpour. Instead of holding outdoor classes, we all gathered under one huge tent. Which leaked. So there we were, sitting in ponchos under a leaky tent with the humidity at 100% and trying to take meaningful notes. Strangely enough, the weather bothered only the trainees; the staff just went on as if it were a beautiful, sunny day.

One of our projects was to make a unique

"camp gadget." We had to think of something none of us had ever seen before. Our Wood Badge Scoutmaster always wore a campaign hat, and since it would be impolite for him to enter our campsite without removing it, we invented the "no-hands campaign hat remover and storage rack." We lashed three poles together (one pole was 18 inches longer than the others and extended above the lashing) to make a tripod. We then took another pole and lashed a shorter one to one end, forming a "Y." The opposite end was lashed (at a right angle) to the pole extending from the top of the tripod. The Scoutmaster would walk into the "Y" as far as he could. If he stooped a little, his hat would rest on the poles and he could just walk out from under it. When he wanted to leave he just reversed the process. We got a perfect score for that one.

Another of our requirements was to make a patrol flag, and woe unto the patrol that had its flag stolen. So, of course, every patrol tried to steal them. But we set our sights higher. We were going to go for the staff flag. We didn't know whether this was legal, but no one had said it wasn't.

We watched the staff flag very closely for

two days and discovered that when the instructor responsible for the flag entered a campsite, he leaned the flag against a tree until he finished his business and then picked it up as he left. Now we made our plans. We would invite this instructor to our campsite for lunch. Since this was a recommended activity, it wouldn't arouse any suspicion.

After lunch, as he was getting ready to leave, two of our guys would get into a discussion with him and walk along with him. This distraction would take his mind off his flag and allow us to grab it. The plan worked perfectly and there was one very embarrassed instructor the next morning as we proudly carried it, along with our own, to inspection.

The last few days seemed to ease up a little, and I still don't know whether that was a planned part of the program or we were just getting used to the routine. As the week drew to a close, we made plans for our overnighter and final banquet.

After dinner on the next-to-last day at camp, each patrol had to leave its permanent campsite and go off to a secluded site to spend the night. It became very emotional because close bonds had developed during the week and it was especially so for me because I was elected Permanent Patrol Leader of the Fox Patrol.

The next morning, we returned to our permanent camp area and started our preparation for the closing banquet. Each patrol was able to requisition food from the quartermaster. The dishes were then prepared and brought to a central dining area, where they were set up in a huge buffet. There were steaks and roasts and fish and turkey and duck and chicken, along with more veggies and breads than I could count. For dessert there were pies and cakes and cobblers of every kind imaginable. We celebrated the conclusion of our training with the greatest feast I have ever seen.

A little over a year later, I completed my ticket (the commitment to put into practice the Leadership Skills taught at Wood Badge) and earned my beads, which were simply handed to me at one of our district's Roundtable meetings.

I never knew there was supposed to be a formal presentation until ten years ago, when my son Randy, who is now an Assistant Scoutmaster in his own son's troop, earned his beads and asked me to present them at his beading ceremony.

Chapter 17.   Camping Merit Badge

Randy had been working very hard to earn his Life Scout rank and was trying to complete all requirements prior to our upcoming Court of Honor. The only thing he needed was the camping merit badge, and he had made his appointment with the merit badge counselor. I drove him to Eric Birch's house, wished him luck, and told him to call me when he was finished. Then I headed for home.

I had barely walked through the door when the phone rang. It was Randy, telling me he was finished and I should come to get him. Nobody passes camping merit badge in fifteen minutes, so I figured he had missed something vital and had been sent home. Too bad he wouldn't have his badge for the Court of Honor.

I started to console him when he got into the car, but he said, "No, Dad, I passed."

I asked him how he could have passed in just a few minutes, and he said that Mr. Birch knew the boys in our troop were always prepared when they came to him so he didn't have to actually test them. He would save the time and just sign the cards. I made him repeat that twice; I couldn't believe what I was hearing.

When my blood pressure returned to normal, I asked Randy what he thought of the process. I was happy when he told me that he didn't agree with Mr. Birch and didn't believe he had really passed.

With only three days until our Court of Honor, I decided to help him out. I called Ron Wagner, a good friend of mine who was also a camping merit badge counselor. I explained what had happened and asked whether he could fit a test for Randy into his schedule. He said that he could, and I had Randy call him for an appointment.

I drove Randy to Ron's home the next day, and more than four hours went by before I got the call to pick him up.

"Well?" I asked as he got into the car.

"I passed" was all he answered until we reached home. Then, as we sat down with a soft drink, he proceeded to describe the testing procedure Mr. Wagner had used and to tell me that this was the most difficult and thorough merit badge testing he had ever undergone. "But now I know that I've earned it," he added as he headed off to bed.

The following evening Randy completed his Scoutmaster's Conference and Board of Review, and the night after that I'm sure I was the proudest parent in the room as I pinned the Life Scout badge onto his uniform.

I have no idea whether Eric Birch ever found out that Randy had been retested, but after we related the incident to our Scoutmaster, his name was removed from our merit badge counselor list.

Chapter 18.   I Want to Be an Eagle

One of my responsibilities in the troop was advancement, and Frank Lawson was probably my greatest challenge. His father, Frank Sr., worked for BSA in the Chicago Area Council, and since the family lived in our Council, he was on our troop committee and Frank Jr. was in our troop. He had been a Life Scout when I joined the troop and now, several years later, he was still a Life Scout.

Since he was so close to achieving the Eagle Scout rank, I tried everything I could think of to prod Frank along, but nothing seemed to work. He loved Scouting and never missed a meeting or a campout, but earning the Eagle rank just wasn't among his priorities. So you can just imagine how pleased I was when he called and told me he wanted to complete his remaining requirements. His father had died two years earlier, and as that anniversary date approached, he wanted to do this in his memory.

Frank needed to complete three merit badges and his service project, which didn't seem to be an overwhelming task until I asked him when he would be 18 years old, the cut-off age for advancement.

There was, as mystery writers like to say, a pregnant pause, and he answered, "Next Thursday."

BSA policy on achieving Eagle Scout rank is very explicit. Unless there are some very extenuating circumstances, everything must be completed by the time the Scout reaches his eighteenth birthday. Period. End of story.

I don't remember how I responded to Frank (which is probably a good thing), but, needless to say, he never achieved the Eagle rank. I happened to run into Frank a few years ago, and he invited me to have lunch with him. He was now an adult, with sons of his own in the Scouting Program. In fact, he was the Scoutmaster of their troop. As we chatted, he told me that not earning the Eagle Scout rank was the greatest disappointment he had ever had.

"I didn't appreciate what you were trying to do for me, Mr. B," he said. "I only hope that there is someone like you in our troop when my boys are ready."

After we said good-bye, I couldn't help thinking that there are still people who believe Boy Scout leaders don't get paid.

Chapter 19. Jamboree 1: Getting Ready

Our Scoutmaster, Carl Thomas, had announced that he wanted to leave the troop after the first boys earned their Eagle badges. When Pat Franks and my son Randy finally achieved that rank, Carl stepped down, and the committee asked me to take the position.

It was now early 1973, and there was going to be a National Jamboree, with three major BSA policy changes. For the first time ever, there would be two locations, the first-class-rank requirement was dropped, and troops could attend as a unit. We didn't want to miss this opportunity, and we decided to make the Jamboree East in Morraine State Park, Pennsylvania, our summer camping activity.

Our entire troop of 28 boys signed up for the trip and since the number of adults required was not quite as strict as it is today, Harold Allen (our committee chairman) and I would be the only leaders going. He was going to make all the travel arrangements and I was to get the boys and equipment ready.

It's a good thing that we had some money in our troop treasury because we needed quite a bit of new equipment. Gasoline stoves and lanterns were no longer permitted, so we had to replace them with propane models. We were also required to have patrol "kitchens," which one of our committee members was able to build for us. And finally, everyone in the troop had to buy a red beret, the official hat of the Jamboree. Unfortunately, the berets did not come with instructions and I'm not sure we ever did get them on properly.

We also needed to build a troop gate that would mark the entrance to our campsite. I had no idea where to begin. The Internet did not yet exist, so I wrote to BSA asking for help and they actually sent me a large packet of photos from previous Jamborees. I gave the pictures to our Senior Patrol Leader, and told him to design our gate, keeping in mind that we had to transport this thing to Pennsylvania.

A few days later, the senior boys came to me with their plans for our gate. It would stand about 10 feet high by 15 feet wide and would support a three-foot replica of our troop patch (which, by the way, I had designed shortly after joining the troop and is the picture on the cover of this book). The final step was to get the materials and assemble the gate in my   backyard.

Everything was now ready, and we still had two weeks to spare.

Chapter 20. Jamboree 2: Getting There

I promised to tell you a little more about Harold Allen, and this is as good a time as any. He didn't have a son in Scouting, but he was totally devoted to the program, anyway. His problem was his volatile personality. He was a good chairman, because everything always got done, but the meetings he ran were the wildest I have ever seen. In the three years I had known him, I don't believe there was ever a unanimous vote. On anything.

Once, when he became ill and was hospitalized, our Troop Committee bought a get well card to send him. As we were signing it, someone wrote "By a vote of 8 to 7" next to the line on the card that said "Get well soon."

This was the man I was going to live with for nearly two weeks at the Jamboree.

When departure day finally arrived, everyone was in the church parking lot, ready and eager to go. We loaded our gear, said our goodbyes and boarded the bus for the long overnight ride to Morraine State Park. At least, that is what I thought.

Several hours into the trip, Mr. Allen asked

the driver what time he expected to arrive in Pittsburgh.

"Why are you interested in Pittsburgh?" I asked him.

"Because that's where we change buses," he answered.

I finally got the whole story. Changing buses in Pittsburgh saved the troop $1,600 (about $53.00 a person). But getting that savings meant arriving in Pittsburgh at 3:00 AM and unloading all our equipment. At 6:30 AM we would have to reload everything onto another bus for the ride to the State Park. And then we would have to do it again on the return trip. I was not a happy camper.

Bus terminals are usually in the grungiest part of town, and the one in Pittsburgh did its part to uphold the tradition. It was nearly 4:00 AM by the time our gear was unloaded and I decided to try to find a diner where we could get a soft drink or a bite to eat.

As we walked through the dark streets, three ladies of the evening came up to me and offered me a group rate. I politely turned them down and told the boys afterward that they were giving me directions to the diner. Some of them even believed me.

The drive from Pittsburgh to the State Park took only a few hours, and once we got there it didn't take us long to set up our camp. As soon as we had finished, I had each boy write down the exact location of our campsite and put it in his pocket before he took off to do some exploring. I'm not sure any of them had to use this note, but none of them ever had trouble getting back to camp.

I made some coffee and Mr. Allen and I sat back and relaxed. We talked about all the activities that the boys could participate in during the week and I actually thought I would enjoy his company.

I was mistaken.

Chapter 21.   Jamboree 3: Start Up

We arrived at the Jamboree a few days before the activities were to start. This gave us time to get settled in and check out our surroundings. On the afternoon of the official Jamboree opening, we were told when and where to assemble and how to join the thousands of other Scouts in marching to the site of the opening ceremonies.

Just before we were to leave, I had all the boys gather under our gate for a group picture. I figured this was as good as they were going to look all week. But before a passing Scouter I had recruited could take the picture, some guy in a blue jump suit asked whether he could be in the photo with us. He looked important so I invited him to join us, and, a short time later, I found out that he was John Warner, Secretary of the Navy. The boys weren't too impressed until I told them that he was married to Elizabeth Taylor.

As we joined the lines of Scouts and Scouters, all I could see were thousands of red berets coming from every direction and all funneling into one huge mass of red. It was one of the most impressive sights I have ever seen.

During breakfast on the fourth day in camp, Mr. Allen came up to me and said, "The boys don't like me." I asked him what had happened and he answered that no one had said good morning to him. I told him that they were probably busy and it was just an oversight but I said I would talk to our Senior Patrol Leader about it.

I forgot all about the incident until the next morning, when I saw Mr. Allen sitting off by himself. As soon as he saw me, he came over and said that now the boys were being disrespectful because every one of them had come up to him and said good morning. This type of complaint became our daily morning ritual and after three or four days, I would have gladly traded him for an eight-year-old Cub Scout.

It didn't take long for the boys to settle into a comfortable camp routine. We would have our breakfast, and immediately after cleaning up, the boys would take off to participate in some of the many activities taking place all around the Jamboree. I wouldn't see them again until lunch. After lunch cleanup, they would disappear again until it was time to prepare for dinner. We usually had some free time after dinner and this was the time that I used to chat with the boys and ask about their day's activities.

One afternoon, just before dinner, I was talking with Randy and asked what we were having to eat.

"You don't need to know that," he responded.

"And why is that?" I asked.

"Because we traded you to another troop for dinner tonight," he said.

It seems that the boys had been encouraged to trade leaders as a way of getting to meet new people. It was a novel experience, both for the other Scoutmaster and for me, and I'm sure I got the better deal. My boys were better cooks than his, but he had to spend the evening with Mr. Allen.

Chapter 22.   Jamboree 4: Wrapping Up

We had been at the Jamboree for about five days when Marv Shore asked for permission to call his mother. He was the youngest boy in our troop, and he had joined only a month before this trip. He was very homesick and even asked to go home. We talked for a while and I was able to get him calmed down and he even seemed eager to remain in camp. I was feeling pretty smug, and I let him make the call, but after he hung up the phone he began crying and once again asked to go home.

Apparently, his mother had cried and told him just how much she missed him and suggested he come home right away. Then his grandmother, who lived with his family, had told him how miserable she was without him and that she missed him and wanted to see him. Finally his mother put the telephone next to their dog's mouth and, when he yelped, told Marv that the dog was crying because he was so lonely. I didn't even want to think about how she made the dog do that, but this time it took me over two hours to get him to agree to stay till the end of the Jamboree.

One of the events used by the Jamboree staff to help boys get acquainted is the "Wide Game." Every Scout is given a letter of the alphabet and told to find boys with the other letters required to spell out a particular phrase. Once they have done this, all the boys find one of the staff, show him their letters, and receive a special segment to add to their Jamboree patch.

In a relatively short time our boys were able to find all the letters they needed—except one. They thought that they might find it at the far end of this huge camp, so they took one of the camp buses to get there. At this point the story gets a little fuzzy because I can relate only what I was told. It seems they spotted a boy with the needed letter, jumped off the bus, took him by the arms and carried him kicking and screaming to the closest checkpoint, where they got their patch segments.

Jamboree week was one of the hottest of the year, with temperatures in the high 90s during the day. We pretty much made our own daily schedules and we all took our showers in the afternoon, just before dinner. The boys' shower facility was very close to our campsite, but the adult showers were about a five-minute walk up a fairly steep hill. One afternoon, the boys came back from their showers in record time. Apparently, several adult Scouters had decided that it was too hot to walk up the hill and had taken over the boys' showers, refusing to let them in.

I finally had a job for Mr. Allen to do. I explained the problem to him and asked him to take care of it. I'm not exactly sure what he said to those Scouters, but there was never a bit of trouble again, and whatever he did, it certainly impressed the boys.

As the Jamboree drew to a close, I started to think about my position with this troop. Harold Allen was really difficult to work with, Randy was talking about moving into Exploring, and my younger son, Scott, had just become a Cub Scout and was three years away from joining the troop. Maybe it was time to move on.

Chapter 23.   A New Troop

We had a troop committee meeting a week after we returned from the Jamboree, and it turned out to be quite unpleasant. Mr. Allen accused me of allowing the boys to be disrespectful to him, and I countered by letting everyone know what a pain he had been. A few minutes later, I resigned as Scoutmaster.

Our District Executive, John James, had approached me several times about starting a new troop. There was another school only a few blocks away, and the school administrators were eager to sponsor a Scout troop. Maybe this was as good a time as any to get it started. So I made the phone call, and in a very short time the plans for the new troop were in place. But there was one small problem. Including Scott, we had only three boys, and we needed five to start a new unit.

"Don't worry about a thing," John told me. "You get the adults to become the committee members we need and I'll care of the rest." And so he did.

We started with those three boys, who were just out of Webelos, and without older, more experienced boys as mentors, I had to teach them everything. I enjoyed every minute of it.

In addition to our weekly meetings, we got together every other Saturday morning and went to the forest preserve to work on outdoor skills. The boys had practiced fire building two weeks earlier and today they were to cook a breakfast. I told them that it had to be a cooked breakfast of at least three items, and they all picked eggs, bacon and toast.

I picked them up at 7:00 AM on Saturday, and we headed to the forest preserve. I told them to build small fires, cook their breakfasts and then show them to me before they ate. Charlie Ceran and Bobby Tyler did very acceptable jobs and were enjoying their meals when Arnie White brought his over to show me. The toast was burned, the fried eggs were rock hard and the bacon had been charred beyond recognition.

"Too bad, Arnie," I told him. "Do you want to try again?"

He turned to me with a puzzled look on his face.

"Why, Mr. B? This is the way my mom makes it and I love it."

He ate it with such enthusiasm that I really believed him. I considered inviting his mother to our next cooking lesson but, since I needed her on the committee, I figured it wasn't such a good idea.

Before our first month was over, each of the boys brought friends, who then brought more friends, and our little troop swelled to nine.

Chapter 24.   We Need Tents

Starting a new troop requires an outlay of money. Tents, cooking kits, lanterns and assorted other equipment have to be purchased. There was no money available from our sponsoring school, so I put up the cash, figuring I would be paid back after our first fundraiser. The tents I bought were a little on the small side, but since the boys were also small, the little tents were satisfactory.

The boys, however, refused to cooperate and in a very short time grew just tall enough that they barely fit inside the tents. I suggested that we raise money to buy new tents by selling candy, but they were really opposed to the idea. Their standard response was, "Cub Scouts sell candy, not Boy Scouts. Our tents are okay." My tent fit me just fine, so I didn't push the candy sale and the boys never complained. But they did continue to grow.

Our District was sponsoring a Merit Badge Camp-O-Rcc, where the boys would have the opportunity to begin work on many different merit badges. Some of these were designed for completion during the weekend. The boys could earn partial credit on certain other badges and complete the unfinished requirements at home.

We arrived on Friday afternoon, set up our campsite, and had a nice dinner. After an hour or so, we all went to bed, looking forward to Saturday morning. Around midnight, the rain started. At first it was a light, gentle rain, but it soon turned into a heavy downpour. Since the boys were packed tightly into their tents, the rain initially came in through the front door. After a short time it also began coming through the tent walls. There wasn't much waterproofing in the tent fabric, and the boys who pressed against the walls created a wicking effect that soaked them and their sleeping bags.

The rain became light and misty on Saturday and the boys had a lot of fun working on their merit badges. They did very well, each of them earning at least two and a few getting some partials to complete later.

Saturday night, though, was another story. The rain was so heavy it made the previous night's storm seem like a drizzle. It was raining just as heavily on Sunday morning, and all events were cancelled. We were told to go home. That was a good thing because the boys and their extra clothing were saturated and they were cold, as well.

Monday evening at our regular troop meeting, they converged on me en masse.

"Mr. B, when can we start the candy sale?"

Chapter 25.   Thirds?

One Monday evening, Mark Sorkin, Larry Friedlander, and Jay Friedlander (boys who were in my former troop) showed up at our meeting and asked whether they could transfer into our troop. They were older than my kids and would be a great addition, but I didn't want to be accused of raiding my former troop.   I thought for a while and told them to discuss it with Mr. Lawson, their Scoutmaster.   And they were also to make sure Mr. Lawson understood that this was their idea.

I was really pleased when they called me the next day to tell me that they had received approval and that I would be getting their advancement records in a few days.

Our candy sale was a huge success, and we were able to buy eight new tents. There was even enough money for the troop to pay back what it owed me. And we got those tents just in time for our first cold weather outing. We started planning for this campout two weeks in advance because I wanted to make sure every boy had adequate equipment.   Mark, Larry, and Jay were a great help with the younger boys, and I felt comfortable taking the whole group on this campout.

My cold weather philosophy was very simple. If it was15°F or above, we went. And unless life-threatening conditions developed, we stayed for the entire weekend. The one exception I made was in our meal preparation. During pleasant weather, each patrol cooked their own meals and any adults on the campout would eat with the boys. The boys were all notified before they went shopping, and the adults paid for their own food, just as the boys did.

In cold weather, though, we switched to troop cooking for dinner, with heavy emphasis on hearty soups and stews that could be served hot.

The weather for this campout was in the mid-20s and actually very pleasant. After lunch we had gone for a 10-mile hike and I was looking forward to a hot dinner. Preparation went well and the flavorful aroma soon had everyone's mouth watering.

Sam Fulton was one of our younger Scouts, and he loved to eat. He was the one who kept checking to see when dinner would be ready and was always first in line if food was involved. So it was no surprise to find Sam waiting with his plate when the dinner call was sounded. Since he was always first, he was nearly always the first one finished and back in line waiting for seconds.

"You know the rules, Sam," I reminded him. "No one gets seconds until everyone has eaten, including the adults."

He reluctantly sat down to wait. After a few minutes had passed, I leaned over to Mark and quietly told him to call thirds.

"Thirds?" he asked. "We haven't had......"

"Shhh," I told him, nodding toward Sam and winking. He got the idea, stood up and called thirds.

Sam jumped to his feet and yelled, "Thirds? We haven't had seconds yet."

"Sure we have," answered Mark. "Where were you?"

Before Sam could answer, the other boys started catching on to the game and joined in. Shouts of "I've had my seconds" and "Me, too," rang out, and poor Sam had no reply. He couldn't believe he had missed a helping and now, to add insult to injury, he wasn't even first in line for thirds. He walked around muttering to himself for the rest of the evening and, surprisingly, the rest of the boys kept the secret.

I sat down with Sam on Sunday morning

and told him about our little joke. He was so happy that he hadn't missed any food that he wasn't even angry. For the rest of the day, I could hear him boasting to the boys that he had been right all along.

Chapter 26.   Duty to Others

Boys with special needs are an important part of the Boy Scouts of America, and a good friend of mine happened to be the Scoutmaster of one such troop. One day he called me and asked whether my Scouts would like to help his kids work on their knot-tying requirements. I told him that I wanted to talk to my boys before making any commitments.

At our next weekly meeting, I waited until the end, when it was time for my Scoutmaster's Minute (a brief thought for the boys to take with them as they headed for home). I was pleased that the boys agreed (even though it was without a lot of enthusiasm), and I decided it would be a good learning experience for my Webelos as well.

The following Saturday morning we all met in a nearby forest preserve, and we had quite a crowd. Besides my boys and the three moms who were our drivers, there were ten additional boys, each with a parent. I got the rope from my car and the boys got started.

The morning's project was to teach the special needs boys how to tie a square knot. My Scouts were going to be the instructors and my

Webelos would work on their own knot requirements at the same time. Most boys can master a simple square knot in less than five minutes; most of the special needs boys needed more than an hour.

This was probably the first time that any of my Scouts or Webelos had spent any time with boys who were a little different from themselves, and their hesitation when they started working was very evident. But Scouting is a great equalizer, and in no time at all the boys were talking and smiling as if they had been lifelong friends. I watched as Scout after Scout took his student's hands to show him exactly where the end of the rope was supposed to go and then gave him a loud "Yesss" followed by a high five when he got it right.

I walked over and sat down to chat with the rest of the adults and then, one by one, each of the boys came running up to show his father his mastery of the square knot. And immediately each boy ran back to his Scout teacher for a big hug. Boys are not overly fond of hugging, even though they tolerate such behavior from their mothers, but these hugs were somehow different. Not one of the Scouts turned away or rebuffed the hugger. And I'm certain that I wasn't the only teary-eyed grown-up in the group that morning.

We repeated this kind of training twice more so that our new friends could learn two more knots. The fall Camp-O-Ree was coming up and we wanted to be sure that they were ready for the competition. After the final good-byes, my boys came up to me, en masse, and told me that they wanted to camp next to these very special Scouts so they could give them a quick refresher before the knot-tying event.

When the Camp-O-Ree arrived and it was time for the knot-tying competition, I couldn't find my boys anywhere. I finally looked over to where our special Scouts were and found my boys acting as personal coaches for their friends. No one cheered louder or harder when these Scouts won a blue ribbon. And then they turned around and gave it to us because we were their friends and we had helped them learn to tie the knots.

Some of these boys taught and some of them learned; it was impossible to distinguish the teachers from the learners.

Chapter 27.   It's Cooked Enough

Several years had passed and my younger son, Scott, was old enough to join the troop. In addition, Jim and Ken Wersching, two brothers who had been in Scott's Webelos den, also became members. Neither these two boys nor I had any inkling that in a few years my wife and I would be divorced, and I would ask their mother out to dinner and end up marrying her.

It was soon time for our Spring Camp-O-Ree, and Mark Sorkin was our troop's Senior Patrol Leader.   Larry Friedlander was his assistant, and Jay Friedlander was a Patrol Leader. These three boys had outstanding Scouting skills and had earned the respect of all the younger boys. I knew we would be ready for the Camp-O-Ree competition.

This competition is very simple. It is a test of Scouting skills, and each patrol functions as a unit. The senior boys who are not in patrols assist in judging and help out wherever they are needed. The competitive events are usually cooking, compass course, knot-tying, lashing and any other skills the organizer wants to include.

One of these tests was a combination of fire

building and cooking. A cord, stretched between two wooden stakes, was placed about one foot above the ground and a second cord about six inches above that. The fire could go only as high as the lower cord, and a pot with water and an egg could go no closer to the fire than the upper cord. This particular activity was timed. The patrol that cooked and ate the egg in the shortest time won the event.

Ken's patrol was having a problem. Their fire was going very nicely, but they couldn't get the water to boil to cook the egg. Ken had been in his patrol for only a short time, but he wasn't about to just stand around and lose a competition.

He walked over to the pot and said, "That looks cooked to me." He reached into the water, grabbed the egg, cracked off the top and swallowed what was certainly a raw egg. "Time!" he yelled to the judge as the other boys watched in amazement.

They didn't score very high in the overall Camp-O-Ree, or even in the cooking event, but one young man earned quite a bit of respect that afternoon.

Chapter 28.   The Black Slime

While I was serving as Scoutmaster, my wife was the leader of my daughter Michelle's Girl Scout troop. One evening I asked her whether she would like to have her girls join my boys on a weekend camping trip to Springfield, Illinois. We would camp overnight in New Salem State Park on Friday and Saturday and tour the historic buildings in Springfield during the day on Saturday. We would return home on Sunday.

My boys liked the idea before I even suggested it to my wife and, in a day or two, her girls and her co-leader also gave their approvals.

We agreed that the boys and I would be responsible for the campfires and the Saturday tour and the Girl Scouts would take care of the meals.

We left right after school for the four-hour drive. As we pulled into the campground parking lot I noticed that there was a State Police car parked there, with two troopers standing next to it. Just as I got out of my car, one of them came over and asked whether I was Larry Bernstein. When I told him that I was, he advised me that my son Randy, who had stayed home to play in a high

94

school football game, had broken his leg during the game. He gave me the hospital telephone number to call so that the emergency room doctors could set the fracture, but when I finally got through, the nurse told me that my sister-in law was already at the hospital and, in my absence, had given permission for the treatment.

Did I feel guilty! First I had missed seeing Randy play and then I wasn't even at the hospital when he had to have his fracture set. Finally, I had to tell him that he would have to spend the rest of the weekend with his aunt and uncle. This was the worst part of the whole incident for Randy because he had lobbied for weeks to be allowed to stay home alone while his mother and I went camping with the Scouts.

By the time I was finished on the telephone, our campsite was set up and dinner was ready. And what a dinner it was. We had chicken, mashed potatoes, veggies and hot rolls. I didn't know whether they cooked it at camp or brought it from home, and I didn't really care because it was delicious. It actually beat hamburger stew in foil, even when it was cooked. Once the cleanup was finished, we all settled in around the campfire. I was ready for a few songs and some of those famous Girl Scout s'mores.

But as the sun set and it got darker, someone yelled out, "How about a ghost story, Mr. B?"

All the kids picked up on this, so with the campfire now down to embers and throwing eerie shadows across the ground, I grabbed another s'more and gave them one of my best.

I told them the very site of our camp had once been a bustling Indian village but had been destroyed as civilization moved west. There had been a great massacre and every man, woman and child had been killed. As the chief took his last breath, he placed a curse on the land his village had occupied and swore that he would rise from the ashes to take revenge on all who settled there, no matter how briefly.

The story went on to tell of the many strange and unexplained disappearances at the campground. The only clue that had ever been found was a trail of black slime leading to and away from the victims. As the story ended, I let the kids sit quietly for a few minutes before telling them that it was late and they needed to get ready to go to bed. I did notice, though, that no one walked alone.

I started to put out the fire while the kids were in the bathrooms brushing their teeth. When you pour a lot of water onto smoldering coals and stir, you get black slime. There was no way I would lose an opportunity like this. I used my shovel to put some of this goop in front of all the tents.

There were two or three boys in each of our small tents, and the girls were all going to sleep together in one large tent. And by the time they were ready to enter their tents, I was back at the fire, making sure it was out and trying to look innocent.

Cries of "There's black slime in front of my tent!" rang out from one part of our camp and were answered by "Mine, too!" from somewhere else.

At first the girls thought the boys had done it and the boys were sure the girls had done it. Then they all got together and concluded that I had done it to scare them. That's what they decided, but then they had to make themselves believe it, and that was another matter.

Suddenly, I heard the sobbing of a little girl. My wife's co-leader had brought her three-year-old daughter, Candy, along and she was terrified and refused to go into the tent.

"No, no, I can't go in there. The black slime will get me."

I knew Candy, so I went over to her, took her by the hand and we went over to the remnants of the fire. I showed her how I had put water on the coals and stirred to make the slime. Then I filled the shovel with the stuff and together we went over to her tent and I showed her how I had put it on the ground. I carefully explained that it was just a joke to scare the bigger kids.

"Now will you go in?" I asked her. She nodded her head, and believing I had solved the problem, I took her back to her mother. Fifteen seconds later her screams let me know that she had not been convinced. It wasn't until I took my shovel and completely cleaned the area in front of the tent that she finally let her mother lead her inside.

I had planned to get up very early in the morning, while all the kids were asleep, to get one of the boys and bring him to my tent. Then I was going to be horrified when he was discovered missing. But after terrifying Candy, I thought that might be carrying things a bit too far. I decided to leave well enough alone.

Chapter 29.   Salamander

Monthly campouts can tend to get repetitive, so I decided to give the boys a treat and take them caving. I called my spelunking friend, Art Schwartz (a little reluctantly, I might add, because I didn't want to get stuck in another rock formation), and made the arrangements for the trip. He even invited the twelve of us to spend the two nights with him in his trailer, never mentioning that his hot water heater had only a five-gallon capacity.

Since we would be getting pretty dirty in the caves, everyone wanted to shower later in the afternoon. We had a quick breakfast and took off for the infamous Trap Door. Art went in first, followed by all the boys. But when it was my turn, I couldn't do it. I've never had phobias of any kind, but my last experience in this cave must have done something strange to my mind. No matter how hard I tried, I just could not lower myself into that hole. Art and the other dad who was with us would have to carry on without me.

They were in the cave for three hours, and for that entire time I sat on the ground next to the opening. In my version of meditation.

When they finally emerged, I decided to make one more attempt to enter the cave. I put my feet into the hole and slowly slid down through the passageway. This was one of the hardest things I had ever had to do, and I was drenched in perspiration by the time I reached the bottom. But as soon as my feet touched the floor, the fear I had been experiencing vanished and I felt fine. There was no need to go any farther, so I climbed out and we all headed to the next cave.

Salamander is more difficult than Trap Door, but it's also a lot more fun for the boys. After you enter the cave you have to either crawl or slither on your belly (depending on the height of the ceiling) for about one quarter mile along the bed of a narrow underground stream. The ground is covered with small rocks and gravel, and by the time you come to the end of the tunnel, you have worn holes in your pants and have a case of hamburger knees.

But it was worth it because we found ourselves in a huge cavern that had to be over one hundred feet in diameter and at least forty feet high. And right in the center was a very large mud hill.

The mud was what I call "clean dirt," since

it was made of earth and water with none of the debris you would find if it were on the surface. Without a word from Art or me, the boys seemed to know instinctively that this was the place to play King of the Hill, and away they went. All the laughter and shouts of pure enjoyment almost made me forget the crawl we would have to make when playtime was over. An hour or so later, we began to make our way back to the cave's entrance.

As we emerged from the cave, I got my first good look at the boys. They were covered in mud from the tops of their heads to the bottoms of their feet. They looked like ten of Uncle Remus's tar babies. Each boy had been told to wear his absolutely worst clothes to explore the cave and to bring along a large plastic bag containing a complete change of clothing.

As soon as we were out of the cave, the boys took off everything they were wearing and put it into their plastic bags (which they could take home to mom or just throw away). They put on their clean clothes and piled into the van for the short ride back to Art's trailer. The one with the five-gallon hot water heater.

Since there was no way the boys could

shower in the trailer, I had to come up with Plan B. There was a garden hose on the side of the trailer so, one by one, the boys stripped down and I turned the hose on them. I had them use soap and then gave them a final rinse before I let them towel dry and get dressed in clean clothes. The water coming out of the hose was cold and not even pizza, pop and ice cream could make up for the icy showers I had subjected them to.

For weeks the boys had been asking to go rappelling, and it wasn't until I promised to take them that we became buddies again.

Chapter 30.   Starved Rock

Now that I was committed to taking the boys rappelling, I figured I had better make sure BSA allowed it. I called my District Executive and, after doing a little investigating, he assured me that there would be no problem as long as we used appropriate safety equipment and had a certified instructor. With Art Schwartz leading our group we met both of the requirements, so I made the arrangements for the troop to go to Starved Rock State Park.

The main bluff attracts most of the visitors to Starved Rock, and activities such as rappelling are not allowed. However, we did get permission to use one of the smaller cliffs, which would give us a vertical drop of about eighty feet. That didn't sound too high–until I stood on the edge and looked down.

We spent Friday night at the park's campground, and right after breakfast Art had the boys practice on one of the small hills. After two hours, we were all ready to go to the top of the bluff to do the real thing. My policy was never to let the boys do something I have not done myself, so I got to be the first one to jump off this cliff.

Art had recruited two of his older Scouts as helpers, and he watched as one of them tied me into the safety harness. Once I was securely strapped in, my harness was attached to the descent rope with the proper number of caribiners for my weight (and for the first time in my life, I claimed a few extra pounds, just to be safe).

The descent rope, which had been tied to two of the largest trees in the area, snaked over the edge of the bluff to the ground, eighty feet below, where the second Scout held onto it. He controlled the rate of descent and could even stop it completely if I panicked and let go of my handhold.

I stood on the edge and leaned into the rope, which easily supported my weight (a pleasant surprise, I might add). It was then that I was supposed to step off the edge, but that was easier said than done. No matter how hard I tried, my legs refused to cooperate and I had to lie down on my belly and slither over the edge.

I couldn't believe it when I opened my eyes and found myself swaying in the air just the way Art had described it. From there, imagining myself a fully armed SWAT officer attacking terrorists, it was only a few seconds until I was on the ground below.

I'm not sure how long the adrenaline rush lasted, but I know I couldn't wait till all the boys had made their descents and it was my turn to go again.

By the way, the boys enjoyed it, too.

Chapter 31.   Who's Bleeding?

It wasn't long after our spelunking trip that Joe Carter, Jerry Barnes, and my son Randy came to me and asked whether we could do it again. Since the troop's program had all been planned I decided to take only those boys, without making it a troop activity.

I called Art Schwartz and arranged to meet him at 8:00 AM Saturday. Since we would need to leave at 3:00 in the morning, Joe and Jerry slept at my house Friday night. The plan was to go caving all day Saturday, spend Saturday night with Art, and return home on Sunday.

When the boys were dropped off at my house, I was pleasantly surprised to see that Jerry's mother had sent along a large chocolate cake for our Saturday night dessert.

At 2:30 on Saturday morning, I woke the boys and we loaded all the backpacks into the trunk of my car. The chocolate cake went onto the deck behind the rear seat for safekeeping. Within five minutes the boys were sound asleep, and away we went.

Somewhere around 6:00 AM we were near Indianapolis, and I started thinking of stopping for breakfast. As I was driving along on the interstate I noticed a car parked on the highway shoulder. It appeared to be abandoned but just as I approached, it pulled out onto the road right in front of me. I swerved into the left lane to avoid a collision with it, but I couldn't avoid clipping the rear of a truck that was in the process of passing me.

We spun around on the highway two or three times and ended up in the grassy median. The boys all said they were uninjured and I didn't think anything had happened to me, either. But just as I was getting out of the car, I happened to touch the back of my head and found that I was covered with something warm and moist. It could only be the blood that was gushing out of my split skull.

I was a bit perturbed that the boys showed no concern until they all came up to me and began pointing at my head and laughing. Apparently, the chocolate cake had flown through the car and hit me in the back of the head. With all the excitement, I never even noticed it. As they helped me clean up the mess, we all agreed that blood had never tasted so good.

We had to cancel our spelunking trip and

find a way to return home. I thought the damage to my car was minimal but both the State Trooper and the tow truck driver told me the frame looked bent and the car was probably totaled. The small town we were in had no car rental agency, so the trooper took us to where we could rent the only vehicle available, a 24-foot U-Haul truck.

We loaded our four backpacks and my spare tire (which I nearly had to wrest away from the tow truck driver) onto the back of this huge truck and headed for home. It's a good thing there were three boys along to keep reminding me I couldn't go through the automatic cars-only lanes as we approached the toll booths.

Chapter 32.   I've Been Robbed

I am not overly fond of having the troop work on a merit badge as a group because a few of the boys usually end up doing most of the work. However, I do make exceptions once in a while. This was the case with the law merit badge. The boys met with an attorney at one of our weekly troop meetings and he assigned work for them to do at home and bring to the next meeting. After four sessions, all the paperwork had been completed.

One of the requirements was a demonstration of the law in action, and I thought this would be a great presentation at our Scout-O-Rama exhibit. Scout-O-Rama was our council's big show, and it attracted several thousand visitors. Nearly every pack, troop and post had a booth that displayed some aspect of the Scouting program. The booths were usually ten feet square, but I managed to secure one of the large exhibit halls for our little drama.

As the visitors came into our hall, I took four of them out of the room, where they couldn't see what the boys were doing, because they were going to be our jury.

My daughter, Michelle, entered the room carrying a purse, and my future stepson, Jim Wersching, snatched it out of her hands and began running as she screamed, "I've been robbed! He stole my purse!"

Jim, dressed in a white t-shirt and jeans, was chased by our police officer and, just as he was about to be captured, pushed the purse into the hands of my son Scott, who was the same size and identically dressed. Of course, the police officer arrested Scott. And Michelle, showing no sisterly love, identified him as the thief.

The four jurors were returned to the courtroom, where they watched as the trial unfolded. Evidence was presented and witnesses were called and, even though due process was probably strained, it really looked like a trial. As it came to a close, the jurors deliberated and found Scott "not guilty."

The robbery and trial were reenacted eight more times over the two days of Scout-O-Rama, and seven times Scott was acquitted. But in the last reenactment on Sunday morning, he was found guilty. It seems we had a hung jury, so they flipped a coin.

I was happy to see the enthusiasm the boys

put into their work and even happier when they received one of the three "Red, White and Blue" ribbons awarded to the weekend's best exhibits.

Chapter 33.   What Else Could Happen?

It was usually pretty hard to get more than one father along on our monthly campouts, but with the weatherman predicting a beautiful autumn weekend, I had three volunteers. That was great, because I could take care of some personal stuff during the day (I was taking dancing lessons with my daughter) and get to the campground much later in the evening.

I went over all the details with Mark Sorkin, my Senior Patrol Leader, and the three adults. I was sure everything would go smoothly, since Mark was experienced and all the dads had been on previous camping trips with the troop.

On Friday afternoon, everyone met at my house to load up the cars with food and equipment. Just before they left, I asked Mark to set up my tent so I wouldn't have to do it when I got there. He assured me that he would take care of it, and the troop took off for Wisconsin and Michelle and I went to our dance lesson.

I got to camp at around 10:00 at night and saw that all the tents had been set up except mine. I was a little disappointed and went looking for Mark to find out why, but he found me first.

"I'm sorry I didn't get your tent up, Mr. B," he said. "I tried, but no matter what I did I always had one pole left over. I tried all different ways, but there was always this one pole left over."

I assured him that I wasn't angry, and I was glad that he didn't stay to watch how I set the tent up, because I had one pole left over, too. I had forgotten to tell him that I kept a spare pole in the bag in case one of the others was lost or broken.

The next morning was one of those dreary, drizzly autumn days that we are all familiar with. The rain isn't hard enough to make you cancel your plans, but it's the kind that gets into your bones so that you never warm up. We were planning to take a 20-mile hike, and this damp weather certainly wasn't going to stop us. Since the three adults were not going on the hike, we decided that they would meet us around lunchtime with something hot to eat.

We had about 15 or 20 cans of soup whose labels had come off during a rainstorm, and we left our chefs with instructions to use their imaginations.

Four hours and about ten miles later, we met up with our traveling kitchen and I have to admit that our unknown soup was delicious. The boys wasted no time in making a game out of identifying the ingredients. The longer they were at it, the sillier they got and the more outlandish the ingredients became. I thought it was pretty funny until they got to the human body parts and then I had to stop the game. I didn't want anyone to think we were a bunch of cannibals.

Now that our stomachs were full, we set off to finish our hike. It wasn't a particularly difficult trail, and since the drizzle had stopped it was actually pleasant walking through the woods. We had been on this trail a year ago, so the boys were watching for the wooden bridge that would let them know there was only a mile to go.

When we finally reached that bridge we faced a real challenge. The bridge was falling apart and didn't look safe to use. The little creek that it spanned was raging and swollen from recent rains and I had no idea how deep it was. Wading across didn't seem to be a good option. It would be sunset soon, and walking 19 miles in the dark to our campsite did not strike me as a better choice. We were going to have to deal with the bridge.

I don't know where I picked up the habit, but I always brought a coil of rope along on hikes, and I was really glad that I had it with me this time. I wanted to test the bridge before sending the boys across, but I knew that if anything happened to me the boys would be alone in the woods, so I asked my son Scott to make the first trip.

I tied the rope under his arms, wrapped it around a tree and slowly let it out as he gingerly took the first few steps. The bridge swayed and creaked but it supported him, and the cheer that erupted when he reached the opposite bank was deafening.

One by one, the boys made the crossing. Finally, it was my turn. I was about halfway across when I heard a sound I had not heard when the boys were crossing the bridge. Just as I turned to look, the boys all started yelling at me to hurry. The bridge supports were starting to come out of the saturated ground.

I had barely reached safety when everything gave way and the bridge fell into the water. All we needed were a few hundred bad guys shooting or throwing things at us, and this could have been a scene in an Indiana Jones movie.

We covered the last mile to our camp very quickly, and the boys immediately started their dinner preparations. It wasn't long before Mark came up to me, asking where I had put the meat for dinner. When I told them that it was in the cooler, they said that they had looked there first but couldn't find it.

"How can you guys misplace all that stuff?" I teased as I went over to the cooler.

But they were right. Apparently, someone had come into our campsite while we were away and helped himself to our ground beef, chicken and steaks. The thief was nice enough, though, to leave all of the vegetables.

I got the boys together and told them that this was now going to be a cooking challenge. We had some soup left over from lunch, plus a few more unopened cans. We also had all kinds of packaged stuff that they could use.

"I'm going to have coffee with the other dads. Call me when dinner is ready," I told them, and I walked away.

It didn't take long for their ingenuity to kick in and I could see them scurrying around and grabbing things to add to the dinner pot. After a while I started to get up to check on what ingredients they were using but then thought better of it and sat down again. Sometimes it's better not to know. At least until after you've eaten.

When we finally sat down to eat, all the boys watched me intently, waiting for me to taste their concoction. I'm not sure whether they were looking for approval or waiting to see whether I would survive. One taste was all it took for them to know it was suitable for human consumption and they wasted no time in following my example. In fact, it was so good that I even had to fight Sam for seconds.

I thought I recognized a few of the items I was eating, so after dinner, while the boys were cleaning up, I wandered over to the garbage bag to look for some clues. There were empty soup cans (unlabeled, of course), plus a number of cans that had contained peas, corn and green beans. There were empty boxes from macaroni and spaghetti, and a few more cans that had held peaches, pears and fruit cocktail. When I found the empty cans of cherry pie filling I knew why the boys had wanted me to take the first taste.

The rain started up again after dinner and we all retreated to the shelter of our tents. By 7:00 it had gotten dark and I was ready to go to sleep. But with the boys still awake, I figured it would be several hours until that could happen. It wasn't long, though, before one of the kids called out to get the time. This was my big chance and I grabbed it.

"It's 10:30," I yelled. "Time to hit the sack."

I never really expected them to take me seriously but they did, and within ten minutes all was quiet in our camp.

Sunday morning I paid the price. I was up at 4:00 AM and sitting with a cup of coffee, when the boys began popping out of their tents. They couldn't figure out why everyone was up so early, until one of the dads accidentally let the truth slip out. It took more than six months for them to let me forget this one.

Chapter 34.　　Klondike Derby

Every winter our district held a Klondike Derby. This event is a competition among patrols and involves many Scouting skills, such as fire–building, cooking, and construction of a winter shelter. The highlight of the day, though, is the great sled race.

Several weeks before the Derby, each patrol is given a suggested plan for the construction of the sled. It isn't required that they follow the plan, as long as the sled meets the minimum length standards and has runners. Wheels, of course, are not allowed. The sled has to carry one person plus a driver and is pulled by a team of sled dogs (the remaining patrol members). Our troop had three patrols entered in the competition.

The first event was the construction of a shelter using only naturally occurring materials. Our boys, as well as all the other Scouts, understood this to mean they should use only items such as fallen trees, branches or snow, and they built their shelters to this guideline. Except for one patrol. Those boys had come across some discarded plywood and plastic sheeting, which they had used to build an outstanding shelter.

And the judges seemed to think so as well, because they gave the shelter a perfect score.

Most Scouts accept the fact that high scores are earned by the best performance, but this time my boys were certain that the judging had not been fair. And they were right. I asked a few of the other leaders how they felt about the judging, and we all agreed that unless someone could show us a plywood tree or a plastic bush, the winning patrol had to be disqualified. It took several hours for the judges to reverse their decision and even though my boys didn't come in first, they felt that at least they had lost fairly.

It was now time for the main event–the sled race. Each patrol had to recruit an adult from another troop to play the role of their seriously injured Scoutmaster. They had to get him onto their sled, transport him for one mile, then stop to prepare a hot lunch. After lunch, the journey would continue for about another mile and would include a river crossing. This "river" was a ten-yard strip marked in the snow. This was probably a good thing because if it had been an actual river, our district would have suffered a very serious shortage of Scoutmasters.

The patrol that picked me did a really good

job during the first part of the race. They had several blankets on the sled, so I was warm enough, and their lunch even included hot soup. However, when we reached the "river," their altruistic mood changed dramatically. They decided that since I was seriously injured they would throw me into the water and, while I was being devoured by the piranhas, they would make it safely across. It was only after I reminded them that they would lose points for arriving at the finish line without a Scoutmaster that they started looking for another strategy.

By doing a little exploring, the boys found a spot where the "river" narrowed and had sturdy trees on both sides. That was when they realized why they had been told to include six-foot staves, rope, and blankets on their sled. With a bit of Scout ingenuity and a lot of Scout bickering, they found a way to get one boy across the river. It was then a simple matter to get their sled to the other side and make a sling for me. I fell in only twice, but since the piranhas were probably eating some other Scoutmaster, I made it to the other side without further injury (that's what they told me to say).

When they finally reached the finish line,

their time was excellent and I was happy to give them high scores for their performance. They came in first in the race and second overall in the Klondike. My troop's patrols, by the way, came in first, third and fourth in the Derby.

Chapter 35. Scout-O-Rama

Scout-O-Rama, our council's annual Scouting show, was one of my favorite events. Since this was 1976, the year of America's Bicentennial, every unit was going to present something special, and I certainly didn't want my boys to be outdone.

In February, the Scout-O-Rama project was the main topic of discussion at our PLC (Patrol Leaders' Council) meeting. Idea after idea was suggested and then discarded, and after two hours or so, we were no closer to a decision than we had been when we sat down. I told the boys to think about this project, and we would try again at our next troop meeting. As they were leaving my home, one of them mumbled, "It's too bad there weren't Boy Scouts in 1776."

"Stop," I said. "I think you've just come up with our answer. Why don't we show what Scouting would have been like if it had been around back then?"

The boys came back into the house, and within 20 minutes Mark Sorkin had developed a plan and assigned tasks to each patrol. One patrol was going to design a uniform and talk my wife into sewing it for them; another was to develop a few merit badges along with their requirements; and I was given the job of obtaining a mannequin of a boy to wear the 1776 uniform.

I had to leave town on a short business trip before I could get the mannequin, but the boys were so enthusiastic about this project they didn't want to wait. They decided my son Scott would make a good interim replacement, and he was the perfect choice to convince his mother to do the sewing. She readily agreed to help and, as the uniform began to develop, probably had even more fun than the boys. Well, at least more fun than Scott, who had to stand motionless as his mother pinned the various pieces of cloth together. He was really happy when I returned home with the mannequin.

It took the boys a while to come up with ideas for merit badges, but once I got them to turn their minds back 200 years, their imaginations took over. They created nearly a dozen badges and then went to work listing the requirements for each. I'm not sure whether the 1776 BSA would have approved of shooting a bear and cooking a bear steak for a camp meal or spending three nights in the woods with nothing but a knife, but how could they not accept "Explain, in detail, the first aid treatment for someone who has been scalped"?

The father of one of our boys was a distributor for a publishing company, and he gave me 25 copies of *Camping Digest* to give away at Scout-O-Rama. Since the boys were having a difficult time designing the actual merit badges, they circumvented the issue by letting visitors to our booth design the badges and then awarding one of the books to a winner every hour. I couldn't argue with that kind of logic and creativity.

I don't know whether it was our exhibit or the chance to win a copy of *Camping Digest*, but our booth was filled with Scouts throughout the entire weekend.

And we won a Blue Ribbon.

Chapter 36.   Rain, Rain, Go Away

Early in 1976, I had started thinking about doing something special to commemorate the Bicentennial, so I asked the boys for some ideas.

I was pleased when they told me that they would like to go to Washington, D.C. I worked up a preliminary budget and met with the parents to discuss the cost of such a trip. They were all very supportive, and I even got two dads to agree to come along with us. We decided to go in August in order to avoid some of the huge Bicentennial crowds.

I met with my three senior boys to plan the nine-day trip. Two hours later, we had decided to make this a camping trip, with stops at Gettysburg, Hershey Park, Valley Forge, and Philadelphia on our way to Washington. We would spend three days in the capital and then take two days to return home. Since there were many details to take care of, we also assigned trip responsibilities.

Mark Sorkin, our Senior Patrol Leader, and his staff would be responsible for getting our equipment ready and planning the itinerary. I would make all the camping and housing arrangements.

A few weeks later, the father of one of the boys called and asked whether I would like to have the boys visit the White House and meet President Gerald Ford. He had a politically connected friend who worked in Washington and could make the arrangements.

Before I could say yes, he also told me that in honor of the Bicentennial the Pentagon was offering tours (this had never been done), and he gave me the telephone number to call to make a reservation. Shortly after this revelation, I read an article in *Scouting Magazine* describing a special Colonial Philadelphia merit badge that could be earned by boys in the Philadelphia Council during the Bicentennial year. I called the Council office and was told that if we visited the historic sites in Philadelphia and completed the written requirements, we could also earn the badge. At the rate I was adding activities, we were going to need a month to make this nine-day trip.

As long as I was calling people and taking care of details, the weeks flew by, but when all preparations had been completed, time seemed to stand still. I was probably looking forward to this trip even more than the boys were.

Charlie Ceran's mother worked for an automobile dealer, and she arranged for us to rent a large van and a station wagon at very reasonable rates. Sam Fulton's mother embroidered one of the neckerchiefs that we would present to President Ford when we made him an honorary member of our troop. And Larry and Jay Friedlander surprised me by showing up at my house with a gate (showing our troop number, city and state) that we could put up wherever we camped.

Both vehicles were in my driveway on the Friday before the trip, and the senior staff came to help get all our tents and equipment loaded. The Scouts brought their personal gear a little later, and they all laughed when I insisted they open their bags and show me their complete uniforms. Even my wife accused me of being an old worrywart–until we found that one boy's uniform was missing. Seems his mom wasn't sure it was clean, so she took it out of the bag and washed it. It was still in the dryer when the boy left his house.

Saturday morning we were ready to go. We had eleven Scouts, one boy still in Webelos (his brother was in our troop, his dad was making the trip with us, and we had one opening), two dads and me, for a grand total of fifteen. This was going to be a driving day of about 400 miles, and I had reserved a site at a campground in Pennsylvania.

Once we arrived at the camp and set up our tents, we had dinner and settled down to enjoy finally being out of our cars. The boys were playing ball when several people came up to them and they talked for quite a while. I had no idea what they were talking about until Mark came over and sat down next to me.

"Those people saw our gate and tents and asked if we were Boy Scouts. When I told them that we were, they asked all kinds of things about our troop and where we were from. We're really on display, aren't we?"

I told him that he was correct and he sat quietly for a few minutes and then left without saying anything. Mark walked over to the other boys and they had a very animated discussion. I watched, slightly confused, as they all went back to the tents and took them down! And then they put them right back up again using a rope as a guideline to make sure that they were perfectly straight.

I didn't say anything to him, but later that evening, as we were getting ready to go to bed, Mark walked over to me and said, "If we're going to be on display, we're going to be perfect."

Boy, I thought to myself, was this ever going to be a great trip!

Our schedule for the next day was to tour Gettysburg, spend the night in Hershey, and visit the chocolate factory in the morning. We thoroughly enjoyed Gettysburg, and all was going according to plan until some storm clouds that had been following us all day finally caught up with us.

The rain started when we were about an hour from Hershey and there was no indication that it was going to let up. Since it was just about time to have dinner, I suggested that we go out for pizza before setting up our tents. I hoped that the rain would let up a little, but I wasn't too optimistic.

Mel Sorkin was Mark's father and one of my closest friends. He continually reminded me how much he disliked organized, uniformed activities, but he was always there for me whenever I asked him to help. As we sat in the restaurant waiting for our pizzas, he walked over and sat down next to me.

"Is the rain bothering you?" he asked. I assured him that it most certainly was.

"Would you like me to stop it?" was his next question. "Sure," I told him. "Go for it."

The next thing I knew, Mel was climbing onto a chair and turning his hand above his head as if he were closing a valve.

"There's a very big pipe in the sky," he said, "and there's this big valve that controls the water that's coming through it. If I close it, the water will drain for a minute or two and then stop."

Mel stood on the chair and continued turning his imaginary valve for what seemed like ten minutes. I noticed that the boys had moved away from us and were pretending they weren't part of our group. I kept watching Mel and trying to think of a way that I could go and sit with the boys. He finally gave one last turn and stepped down from the chair.

"It will just be another minute or so," he said. Then he sat down, and placed his wristwatch on the table in front of him. And in one minute the rain stopped and the sun came out.

The boys looked at each other and then at

me.

"How did he do that?" they all asked.

"Right," I said and turned to Mel. "How did you do that?"

All I got from him was that he had closed the valve, and to this day, nearly 36 years later, he still won't tell me.

Chapter 37.   Saved by the Navy

With our stomachs full of pizza and the rain off somewhere else, we set up our camp. The next morning was glorious, without a cloud in the sky, and I made a mental note to bring Mel along on more of our campouts (especially if rain was in the forecast).

Everyone enjoyed touring the Hershey chocolate plant, and even those of us who were not chocoholics had trouble resisting the call when the tram let us out at the chocolate-filled gift shop. From there it was off to Valley Forge and then to Philadelphia, where we would tour the U.S. Mint, stop at the Liberty Bell, and visit the historic sites that were required to earn the Colonial Philadelphia merit badge.

By Tuesday evening, our uniforms were getting a bit fragrant and I figured this would be a good time to visit the laundromat. Tom Bernier, the other father along on the trip, took two boys and all the uniforms and went off to get them washed.

They returned an hour or so later with the neatly folded clothing, and the boys had no trouble identifying their shirts, but the pants were another story. We sorted the boys by size and weight and then tried to match the trousers to their owners. But every time we thought we had the pants and Scouts matched, one boy would wail, "These aren't mine." If I had had a video camera with me, I am certain I would have had a winning entry in a comedy competition.

The following morning we left for Washington, D.C., and Andrews Air Force Base, where we would spend the next three days. Like nearly all military bases, Andrews allowed Boy Scouts to camp on their grounds at no charge. The base had an area where we could set up our tents and would provide us with drinking water. The normal temperature for Washington in August is in the 90s, and I didn't think President Ford would be too happy to meet us after three days without showers.

After considerable pleading on my part, the youth liaison officer finally suggested that I contact the Navy. It seems they rent space from the Air Force and have a dormitory available for youth groups. The Navy officer I spoke to not only arranged for us to stay in an indoor facility with showers, he also offered to let us eat in their mess hall for just a few cents a meal.

Another troop of Scouts was also staying in the dormitory, but other than casual greetings we didn't have much contact with them. Until breakfast on our second day. We were walking toward the mess hall, when the other troop went running past us, making the kinds of noises that young boys are well known for.

Mark watched them race past us and then told our boys that we were going to show people how Scouts were supposed to act. He lined them up by twos and quietly marched them into the mess hall. I didn't think anyone else noticed, but as we went into the building, the seaman taking our tickets looked at the other troop and then at ours.

"Nice kids," he said to me.

Chapter 38.   Where's Bobby?

I was really looking forward to our meeting with President Ford and, when the time for our visit to the White House finally arrived, I was more excited than the boys were. We went to the special entrance and gave the guard our pass. He showed us where to wait and in a few minutes a young lady, who introduced herself as one of President Ford's secretaries, gave us the bad news. The President had been nominated for another term at the Republican National Convention, and without any regard for us, had gone to Kansas City to accept.

She took the neckerchief (making him an honorary member of our troop) on his behalf, posed for all kinds of pictures with us and gave us a special tour of rooms in the White House that are not open to the public. We were all disappointed and I vowed never to forgive the President and surely never to vote for him. However, two weeks later I received a letter from him, thanking us for the neckerchief and telling us how much it meant to him. All was forgiven, but I still didn't vote for him.

We squeezed every activity possible into

the three days we spent in Washington, including as many evening events as we could find. On our last night we took a boat trip on the Potomac River to Mount Vernon and didn't return to our dormitory until rather late.

The Scoutmaster from our neighboring troop was waiting for me and asked me to drive him to the motel where his troop's bus driver was staying. They were missing a boy and he thought they might have left him on the bus.

The motel was only a few minutes away and when the driver opened the bus, there was Bobby, sound asleep on the back seat. He had stretched out to rest as they drove back from dinner and dozed off. It wasn't until an hour or so later, when the boys were ready to go to bed, that anyone even noticed he was missing. He never fully woke up as his Scoutmaster guided him to my car and then into their dormitory room. He thanked me and I didn't give it any more thought.

Saturday morning, as we were packing up our gear to begin our trip home, Bobby came up to me and asked if he could talk to me.

"Sure" I said, sitting down. "What's on your mind?"

"Did I fall asleep on our bus last night?" he

began. "Did you and Mr. G have to come and get me? The guys all said you did."

Bobby was one of the smallest boys in his troop and I was pretty sure that he got teased a lot, so I decided to stretch the truth a little and help him out.

"Absolutely not," I told him. "I don't know what you're talking about."

His face lit up as he said, "I knew it was a joke all along, and the guys even got Mr. G to go along with them." He was grinning from ear to ear as he left to go back to his troop.

After the excitement of our trip, the ride home was a little subdued. The boys all completed the written requirements for the Colonial Philadelphia merit badge, and I mailed the requisite materials, including the applications, to the Philadelphia Council office. I received the badges just in time to award them at our Court of Honor.

I later found out that we were the only Scouts in the country, outside of the Philadelphia Council, to have earned this particular merit badge.

Chapter 39.   Owasippe

As another spring rolled around, I began to make plans for a one-week stay at summer camp with the boys.

One evening, my wife and I were having dinner with our friends Eddie and Bobbie Ginsberg, and I lamented that with only seven boys in our troop, I couldn't get another dad to go to camp with me and so we would only be able to go for one week. Eddie was one of my best friends and, in fact, he and Mel and I had all gone to high school together and had remained close friends ever since.

Eddie was also a Scoutmaster, and he always liked to remind me that when he was first recruited to become a Cubmaster, he had asked me how much of his time it would take and I had told him that it would take only an hour a week. Of course, I deny saying any such thing.

Anyway, Eddie also had a small troop of seven boys and he and I were in the same predicament. So we came up with the great idea of combining our troops for two weeks at Camp Owasippe, with each of us being there for one week.

We decided to take the boys on a joint campout for a weekend to see how they would get along and then propose our summer camp idea. The campout was a great success, and the boys unanimously voted for the combined summer camp proposal. Eddie and I then went to our respective troop committees and, since they had no problem with the proposal, we started arranging the details.

I was going to take the first week and Mark Sorkin, my Senior Patrol Leader, would be leader for the entire troop for that week. Eddie would take over for the second week and his son Marc, who was the Senior Patrol Leader of his troop, would have the position for the second week.

Eddie made the reservations, since his troop was based in Chicago and Owasippe was a Chicago Council Camp. He also arranged for the boys to travel to camp on the Council bus. He and I would each drive our own cars so that we would have one in camp in case of any emergency.

The boys and I arrived at camp at about the same time in the early afternoon, and it didn't take long for us to get set up. While we were working, a group of eight to ten boys came into the adjoining campsite. The Chicago Council had

140

invited them to spend a week in camp to try out the Scouting program, hoping that some of them would like the activities enough to join one of their neighborhood troops. They had no leader, but a camp commissioner had been assigned to them to guide them along. My kids waved and said hello and they did the same, and I didn't give the matter any more thought.

The next morning, though, was another story. Some of my boys came into camp soaking wet and finally told me that a few of our neighbors had doused them with buckets of water when they walked across a corner of their campsite. The unofficial camp tradition was that you could splash someone walking through your camp without permission, but tossing full buckets of water seemed like overkill.

I figured that if I didn't do something to defuse the situation, we would have a terrible week, so I told Mark to invite the neighboring boys to our evening campfire. Everyone was a little tentative at first, but cobbler and ice cream works wonders on kids, and before the evening was over they were all best buddies. No one ever got splashed again, and I'm sure that the two groups learned a lot from each other.

A variety of activities were available to the boys, and I let them pick the ones they wanted to try. They decided on an overnight canoe trip, an overnight horseback trip, and an overnight wilderness survival experience. Since I was there first, I picked the overnight canoe trip for my week and left the other two for Eddie to deal with.

Chapter 40. You're Getting Very Sleepy

When I was in college, I had learned the basics of hypnosis, and I made the mistake of sharing this fact with some of my boys. Here at camp, they kept asking for a demonstration, and after four or five days I finally gave in and agreed to show them how it worked. Looking back, I'm sure that it was not one of my better ideas. But it happened, so it's included in this book.

Hypnosis is, in its simplest form, a technique for convincing a subject to accept suggestions from the hypnotist.   It is not dangerous, and individuals who are hypnotized will not do anything that is contrary to their morals or beliefs.   Furthermore, should the hypnotist vanish from the face of the earth, all the hypnotic suggestions will disappear in an hour or two.

As the boys, including the neighboring kids, gathered around, I used the power of their minds to see which of them would be the most susceptible to hypnotic suggestions. I had them lace their fingers together, turn their hands so that the palms were facing outward and close their eyes.   Then I had them imagine that I was wrapping their hands with a steel cord. When I told them to open their eyes and take their hands apart, three of the boys had quite a difficult time until I told them that I had loosened and removed the cords. Little did they know that they were going to be the subjects of my demonstration.

We started with a few simple suggestions, such as having their chairs get too hot to sit on and getting a shoe stuck in a large wad of gum.

Then I told Scott Greenenwald that he had misplaced his belly button. He immediately pulled up his shirt to check for himself, since he was not going to take my word for something so important. Once he realized that it was indeed missing, he didn't get upset but he wanted it back. After a few minutes one of the boys took a piece of paper, drew a circle on it and wrote Scott's Belly Button under the circle.

"Here's your belly button, Scott," he said.

"Thanks," Scott answered, stuffing the piece of paper under his shirt. Then he sat down to watch someone get hypnotized.

Mark Sorkin was next. I told him that he was on the moon and the people who lived there spoke only the moon language. Luckily, his traveling companion was fluent in moon and would be able to translate for him. Through his interpreter, Mark had a rather long and involved conversation with several moon people. Among other things, he assured them that since no one on earth knew of their existence, he would never tell a soul what he had seen.

My third subject was Jerry Crandall, one of our neighbor boys. He insisted that he could never be hypnotized but he was actually the most receptive of the three boys I worked with. I put him to sleep and told him that when he awoke every boy in the entire camp (except for him) would be wearing nothing but his underwear.

When he opened his eyes, there was an unbelievable look of astonishment on his face. His friends tried to get him to remove his clothes and join the group but he wouldn't have any of that.

"You're an adult," he said to me. "Tell these kids to get dressed."

After a few minutes, I did as he asked and he was very visibly relieved.

When my little show was over I spoke to the boys to be sure that they were feeling okay. They wondered why I was concerned; after all, they had not been hypnotized.

Chapter 41.   The Indian Burial Ground

It was a gorgeous summer morning when we set out on our canoe trip. The total trip was about thirty miles down a slow-moving and winding river. We would travel a little over twenty miles the first day and then spend the night on a sandy beach the camp had nicknamed the Indian Burial Ground. I was pretty sure the boys would want to hear a story about how the camp got its name, and the long ride gave me enough time to think of one.

Once we reached the beach, we unloaded our gear from the canoes and the boys got a chance to swim and work off some of the energy that had been building up during the day. By the time we finished dinner, the sun had set and the only light we had came from our flickering campfire.

It wasn't long before they were asking for a ghost story, and I had the perfect one ready for them. (I have a limited repertoire of "Indians coming back from the grave" stories, so this one was a lot like the one about the black slime).

I told them that the very spot where we would spend the night had really been a sacred burial site for the Indians living there before the coming of the white man. The Indians were forced to relocate but could not take the bones of their ancestors with them.

With strangers walking across their graves, the spirits could not rest, and if you listened carefully you could hear their voices in the night. The tribal Medicine Man had then cursed the land and all who set foot upon it and vowed to take his revenge by killing trespassers as they slept and removing their heads. I was happy that none of the boys asked why the Scouts kept coming back to this beach if it was so dangerous, because I didn't have a good answer.

I went on with my story for nearly an hour, and the fire was down to glowing embers by the time I had finished. As the boys went off to their tents, I could see them looking all around and trying to find reasons not to go to sleep.

I woke up during the middle of the night to the sounds of voices whispering and laughing, and for a brief minute I nearly believed my own story. It wasn't until I asked some of the people who had been coming to Owasippe for years that I found out that the bluff above our beach was the local lovers' lane, and the voices belonged to teenaged couples.

When the boys got up in the morning I overheard them asking whether anyone else had heard the voices and then I even saw someone taking a silent count to be sure everyone was present. They rushed through breakfast and I didn't have to call them twice when it was time to start the last part of our trip. Quiet boys on a canoe trip are pretty spooky, and I was happy when they got back to their normal noisy selves.

It was raining when we reached the end of the trip and I had Mark take the boys to a sheltered spot while I called the camp to send a truck to pick us up and return the canoes. It caught me by surprise when the waterfront director said he didn't know who I was and had no record of our being in camp, let alone on a canoe trip.

We went on like this for ten minutes until I offered to sell the canoes and use the money to hire transportation to take us back to the camp. Now that I had their attention, they checked a little deeper and we all found out that Eddie had us registered under his troop number and I was using my troop number when I talked to them. It didn't take long for the bus and canoe trailer to show up and take us back to camp.

Last year I was talking to Mike Ginsberg, Eddie's younger son, about some illustrations for this book and as we chatted this canoe trip came up. He told me that nothing had ever scared him more than my story and, in fact, his brother Marc, who was sharing a tent with him, had moved his sleeping bag so that he could put his legs on top of Mike's.

When Mike asked him what he was doing, Marc said that if the Indians came to behead one of them, the other would wake up and could help.

Chapter 42.   Where's the Doctor?

Camp Owasippe offered a wide variety of merit badges, and David Stein and my son Scott took advantage of the opportunity to work on horsemanship. The stable was several miles away, so every afternoon I would drive the boys there and pick them up two hours later.

One day, Mark Sorkin asked to use my car so he could drive the boys to their lesson. He had recently obtained his driver's license and, since the entire trip was on camp property, I let him do it. To keep the driving to a minimum on his first trip, he was going to stay at the stable until Scott and David were ready to return to camp.

About an hour after the boys left, my camp commissioner came running up to me and told me to get to the stables as soon as I could because there had been a bad accident and one of the boys was seriously hurt. He didn't have any more information but said that he would keep an eye on my kids while I was gone.

The Scoutmaster in a neighboring campsite had a car and while he was driving me to the stable I was haunted by the fact that I had done something really dumb and because of it there was a badly injured boy.

An ambulance had already arrived and I could see two paramedics, the merit badge counselor, and several stable workers huddled over a boy on a stretcher. One of the paramedics came over to me and told me that a horse had trampled David and they believed he had broken ribs and a punctured lung. They were going to take him to the hospital, which was about 35 miles away, for emergency surgery.

I went over to see David and was very surprised that he was trying to sit up on the stretcher and look around. I was even more surprised when he said he felt fine. I'm not an expert, but he certainly didn't look like a boy who had been trampled. I got Mark and Scott together to see whether they could shed a little more light on the accident.

Apparently, one of the horses had started walking away from the boys and David went over to get the reins. Just as he took hold of them, he tripped and fell and the horse put one hoof down on his chest. When he felt the boy under him he immediately lifted it off but, in a moment of panic, David had yelled that the horse had stepped on him and someone overreacted and called 911.

I was certain that David was not injured but decided to let the paramedics take him to the hospital, just in case there was some injury that wasn't visible. Mark and Scott went back to camp with our neighboring Scoutmaster and I followed the ambulance to the hospital.

By this time David was having a grand old time with all the attention, and it was nearly impossible to keep him from sitting up. An hour later, the emergency room doctor confirmed my suspicions and told me that David was fine and that he could go back to camp.

When we got back to Owasippe, David told his story over and over again to all the boys who would listen, and each time it got a little better. By the time he was ready to go to bed, he believed that he had single-handedly captured a herd of wild horses and fought them off when they turned on him. Personally, I was looking forward to some coffee and a munchie later that evening.

I had barely gotten comfortable when my son Scott came up to me, gasping for breath.

"I can't breathe," was all he was able to say.

I had him sit quietly while I tried to locate the camp doctor or nurse but it was nearly 10 PM and they were nowhere to be found. Scott had a history of hay fever, but he had never experienced anything like this. It looked as though he was going into a full asthmatic attack and, without any medication available, I became very concerned.

After resting for a few minutes his breathing improved but I still thought it would be a good idea to have him seen by a doctor. The only medical care was 35 miles away at the same hospital I had been to earlier, so I got someone to watch my kids and Scott and I left for the hospital.

By the time we got there, Scott was considerably better and I'm sure that the doctor thought I was abnormally overprotective. After all, who else would drag healthy boys into an emergency room? As for Scott, he had been running in the woods and the damp night air had caused a brief asthmatic episode. Had I kept him quiet for an hour or so, he would have had a full recovery on his own.

To recap, I had a near panic attack when I thought one of my boys was badly injured. I missed dinner and some badly needed snacks and I took two 70-mile round trips to a hospital and didn't get to bed until nearly 1 AM.

Just a typical day in the life of a Scoutmaster.

Chapter 43.   Changing of the Guard

Even with all the activities that were going on at camp, I found the whole experience very restful and always had an hour or so during the day to put my feet up and relax.

Except, of course, for August 16, 1977. This was the day that Elvis Presley died, and the entire camp went into mourning. Even my best fruit cobbler didn't work on my kids, and it wasn't until the next morning that they began to behave normally again.

As my week drew to a close, I secretly hoped that Eddie wouldn't show up so I would be forced to stay. But on Sunday morning, right on schedule, he drove up and he even remembered to bring Bobbie along so I would have company on the long ride home. I got him a cup of coffee and we sat for a while as I filled him in on everything that had happened during the week. Somehow, though, I just happened to forget about the two overnighters that I had saved for him.

As I was getting ready to leave, I realized that I had nothing to wear except my uniform. After a week of kid food, I wanted to stop and have a real dinner on the way home, and I asked

Bobbie whether it would bother her to be seen in a restaurant with an overgrown Boy Scout. It was a good thing it didn't, because I would have hated to leave her in the car while I ate.

After Eddie's week was finished, we got together to review the overall camp experience. He had a much better memory than I did, because he didn't forget to let me know exactly how much he had enjoyed his two overnight adventures.

Our kids had made new Scout friends, they had taken three overnight trips, and they had earned a grand total of sixty merit badges. They all survived the Indian Burial Grounds and a few of them got to visit a hospital emergency room.

And then there was Lenny Foster.

Lenny was the only boy who did not earn even one badge. He was the boy who used over 200 matches trying to light the fire required for the cooking merit badge, and he was the boy who found a stray cat and wanted to adopt it. Eddie drew the line at that one.

On the last Sunday before heading for home, Eddie passed out all the completed merit badge cards to the boys. A few minutes later he found Lenny sobbing in his tent and, assuming that he was crying because he had not earned any badges, went in to console him.

After a few minutes of getting Eddie's best fatherly and Scoutmasterly effort, Lenny looked up and said.

"Merit badges? I don't care about any merit badges. I want to take the cat home and you won't let me."

Eddie had a hard time keeping a straight face as he walked away from Lenny.

Chapter 44.   I'm My Own Grandpa

Summer camp at Owasippe turned out to be one of my last activities with the troop. I got divorced and needed some time to get my personal life back in order. I wanted to step down as Scoutmaster, but I couldn't get anyone else to take the job. After trying for over a year to find a successor, I finally just had to leave. Within a short time, the troop disbanded. My son Scott was now a Life Scout, and I wanted to do whatever I could to help him earn the Eagle Scout rank.

We both joined another troop in the neighborhood, but three months later our Scoutmaster had to step down because of ill health. As Committee Chairman, I tried to keep the troop together until a new leader could be found, but most of the boys transferred to other troops and ours disbanded.

Scott seemed to lose interest in Scouting at this time, and it took all my persuasive powers to get him to make one more try. We found a small troop, and we both joined. Scott worked on his Eagle requirements and I was an Assistant Scoutmaster. I had remarried by this time and, after a month or two of seeing me go to the weekly meetings, my stepson Ken (who had dropped out of Scouting several years earlier) asked to join our troop.

Ken also got his dad involved, and since he had also remarried, his stepson, Jay, joined the troop, too. It wasn't long before my nephew decided he wanted to be a Scout as well, so I had one more family member in our troop.

When Scott finally earned his Eagle Scout rank, the Court of Honor was like a disjointed family reunion. In fact, the mother of one of the boys (one of the few not related to me) went up to my wife and asked her to explain how everyone was related. Dawn very carefully identified each person and how they fit into the family picture. By the fourth or fifth name the woman's eyes glazed over and she kept nodding and saying "uh-huh" until she finally walked away shaking her head and mumbling under her breath.

Just in case all the relationships aren't clear, here is a scorecard of attendees.

We had my son Scott, the new Eagle Scout, my older son Randy (Eagle Scout) and my daughter Michelle (Girl Scout). There was also my wife Dawn (troop treasurer), my ex-wife Jan (Scott's mother), and my two stepsons, Ken (a

Scout) and Jim (a former Scout).

Then there was Bob (Dawn's ex-husband and troop committee chairman), Charlotte (Bob's wife and troop committee member) and Jay (a Scout and Charlotte's son).

In addition there was Gail (Dawn's sister and committee member), Steve (Gail's husband and committee member) and their son Scott (Scout).

And completing the group were Todd (Scoutmaster) and Brandon, Bobby, Keith, Stuart and Mike (all Scouts), who weren't related to me.

It's probably a good thing my other three nephews didn't want to join the troop, too.

Chapter 45.   Let's Go Rafting

After all the summer activities, I thought it would be a welcome change to take Scott, Jim, and Ken on a little camping trip where they wouldn't have to work on advancement or any other Scouting tasks. Since it was going to be a fun trip, my wife and my daughter, Michelle, also came along.

The campground we selected was in Wisconsin, about 350 miles away, and it had a lot of things for the kids to do. In addition, there was a river with fast water about 100 miles from the campground, and several outfitters offered rafting trips. As soon as we set the date for the trip, I made a reservation for rafting at Joe's Peshtigo River Raft Trips.

Wednesday was a beautiful sunny day, and I was eager to get started. We left at 9:00 AM, and with one stop for lunch, I figured we would arrive at Joe's just in time for our 1:30 PM reservation. As we drove through the Wisconsin countryside, I'm certain there were billboards advertising Joe's raft trips every ten miles or so. Traffic was light, and it was about 12:30 when I saw the sign telling me to turn left for Joe's

Peshtigo River Raft Trips.

I made the left turn and, spotting several racks loaded with yellow rubber rafts, I turned into the driveway and parked. Since there was plenty of time, I had everyone put on life jackets and helmets and pose for pictures next to the rafts. When I finished I went inside to check in and pay for our excursion.

I couldn't believe it when the attendant told me that they did not have our reservation and, in fact, didn't even have a 1:30 rafting trip. He also had no record of the credit card deposit I had given him more than a month ago. There was room for us on the 2:00 trip, so I paid and figured I would straighten out the deposit with my credit card company. It seemed that Joe ran a pretty sloppy business and I hoped we wouldn't be disappointed with the trip.

I went outside to wait and was in the process of telling Dawn what had just happened when the attendant came looking for me.

"You made your reservation with Joe's, didn't you?" he asked.

"Of course I did," I answered and I was just about to ask whether he had lost my reservation again when he took the wind right out of my sails.

"We're Wild Water Rafting," he said, chuckling under his breath. "Joe's is a half mile down the street. Come back inside and I'll call and check it for you."

It took only a few minutes to verify that I was in the wrong location, and now I had to go outside and tell the group to take off their life jackets and helmets and get back into the cars so we could get to the place where we belonged.

And that wasn't even the worst part, because there were about thirty people waiting to leave for their trips, and they had all heard the story. I could hear ripples of laughter all the way to Joe's.

One of the things I've learned from working with kids is that they absolutely never forget a grown-up goof. And it goes double when Dad is the one who goofed. It's been over 25 years since this happened, but any time I'm with Scott or Michelle or Jim or Ken and the word *river* or *raft* comes up in conversation it's always, "Hey, Dad, remember when you took us to the wrong raft place?"

Chapter 46.　　After the Bunny Hill

The boys had been asking to go skiing ever since the weather turned cold, and Todd Bender, our Scoutmaster, finally agreed that a ski trip should be our January outing. Since we were able to rent a very large cabin just a few miles from the ski slopes, the committee decided to make this a family affair. I had never been on skis but I figured that there had to be small hills for beginners and I was in reasonably good shape for an old guy, so how bad could it be?

Our group of six boys, two leaders, and four parents arrived at the cabin late Friday evening. The boys went right to bed but one of the moms made a pot of coffee and the adults stayed up swapping war stories into the wee hours. Unfortunately, the coffee was not decaffeinated, and the five or six cups I drank had me wired and ready to hit the slopes. All night long.

Since all the boys and five of the six adults were new to skiing, we decided it would be a good idea to get a lesson before starting out. After this lesson, which was much too short to suit me, the boys took off and within minutes were flying down the slopes. I decided to be a bit more conservative and headed to the bunny hill. After all, older bones take a long time to heal.

I should have realized that I was not cut out for skiing when it took me nearly two hours to master the intricacies of the bunny hill. I really wanted to ski in a southerly, downhill direction but my left ski headed east while my right ski went off to the west, making me slide down the hill on my backside. But I finally conquered the bunny hill, and that was my undoing.

"Where is the next hill?" I asked the young woman who looked after the unfortunate souls still struggling on the bunny hill.

"Right over there," she answered, pointing off somewhere to the left.

Maybe it was the cold air or the leftover caffeine or the thrill of mastering the bunny slope, but without thinking, I got onto the ski lift. Before I knew what was happening, I found myself looking down from the top of a mountain. A really big mountain.

At that moment I realized that I had been sent to the next *closest* ski run and not the next *ability level* hill, which was what I wanted. I also discovered that there is only one way down. I decided to take a minute to consider my options.

I could stay on the top of the mountain until spring and walk down on the grass or I could try to ski down. Neither of those was particularly appealing and since there was another four months until warm weather, I chose the latter option. I tried to remember what the instructor had told us during our lesson, as well as what I had learned on the bunny hill. Finally, I took a deep breath, pushed with the ski poles, and down the slope I went.

Something of what I had learned must have sunk in because I was actually skiing down the hill. For about 15 feet. And then I became airborne (as in head over heels) and tumbled through the snow for what seemed like an eternity.

I finally came to rest in a snow bank and was ecstatic when my quick self-examination didn't find any broken bones. The only thing damaged was my dignity and that wasn't helped when all the boys came skiing down the hill yelling "Hi, Mr. B" as they sailed by.

As I struggled to remove my skis, I wondered whether a St. Bernard with a flask of hot chocolate (Scout leaders don't drink brandy when they are out with the boys) would find me if I just stayed where I was. I gave up on the St.

Bernard rescue just about the time I got the skis off and decided to walk down the remainder of the hill. And that was not an easy task in ski boots.

When I finally reached the bottom, everyone in our group was waiting, since it was just about time to head for home. As we walked towards our cars, the boys thanked us for taking them and said that they had had a great time. And they wanted to do it again.

I figured I would take a pass the next time. Unless, of course, they could guarantee that the St. Bernards would be on duty.

Chapter 47.   Hold That Pose

As another summer rolled around, our troop made plans for a trip to Colorado instead of a local camp. We drove to Colorado Springs and planned to set up camp at the Air Force Academy for three days while we went sightseeing. The Air Force Academy provided drinking water but nothing else, and I figured that we would be pretty ripe after three days without showers.

I knew that every military installation had a youth officer, so I went to find him. He was very understanding and gave us permission to use the showers in the men's gymnasium, provided we finished by 7:00 AM. This was easier than I thought, so I tried to get permission to also use the pool. That was a much tougher sell, and I made a quick withdrawal before he changed his mind about the showers.

While we were in Colorado we did all the normal things, such as trips to Pike's Peak, the Royal Gorge and all the other places tourists want to see. One evening we went to the beautiful Seven Falls.

To properly experience the falls, you have to take an inclined railway car several hundred feet up the side of the mountain. From there you climb about 300 stairs and finally reach a viewing area where you can see the seven illuminated waterfalls. You can also look across the valley to the next mountain, and that's when I saw this magnificent bighorn ram, just standing there and waiting for me to take his picture.

I had only my 50mm lens with me, and I really needed a telephoto lens to do justice to this great animal. I told Todd Bender (our Scoutmaster) that I was going to the car to get my lens, and away I went. Down the 300 stairs, down the inclined railway, and about one-half mile to the car. I reached for the keys and that's when I realized that this wasn't my car and the keys were still in Todd's pocket. So I turned around and ran the half-mile, went up the inclined railway and climbed the 300 steps.

Todd had a huge grin on his face as he dangled the keys in front of me. I looked across the valley and couldn't believe my luck when I saw the ram still standing there.

Down the 300 stairs I went one more time. Then I rode down the inclined railway and ran the half-mile to the car. I got my lens and, after making sure I wasn't locking the keys in the car, I started back. A bit slower this time, I might add. Across the parking lot and walkway, up the inclined railway, and back up the 300 stairs. By this time, I was gasping for breath, but there he was. Standing perfectly still and probably thinking, "When will this jerk finally take my picture so I can leave?"

I put my telephoto lens on the camera and took several pictures, amazed at how lucky I was that he had not moved away. As I started to walk towards our group I overheard a man tell his companion to take his binoculars and look at this *statue* of a bighorn sheep.

I couldn't believe what I was hearing as he described the cracks he could see on the body. I asked to borrow his binoculars, hoping I would see my ram socializing with a statue. But no such luck. I had made two breathless round trips to the car, scaled hills and stairways, and nearly had a heart attack–to photograph a statue.

Chapter 48.   Pinewood Derby

Shortly after returning from our trip to Colorado, I left the troop to become a Unit Commissioner. It took me a while to get used to this job because I was now working with unit leaders instead of boys.

After taking Commissioner Basic Training, I was assigned a troop and a pack. They were both sponsored by the same elementary school, and many of the parents had boys in both units. This made it pretty easy to get to know them and I enjoyed this change from the Assistant Scoutmaster duties.

My pack's Cubmaster called to ask me to take charge of weighing the boys' cars at the upcoming Pinewood Derby (he must have read my Scouting résumé and noted that I had almost served as a Pinewood Derby Chairman).

A Pinewood Derby consists of two parts. First, it is a joint parent-son project to carve a racing car out of the block of wood that is given to them. There are no rules regarding how the car is to look or how it is to be painted, and our pack, like most, had prizes for many categories and styles.

The second part of the event is the race. The boys compete against each other in several heats until the overall winners are determined. Every boy who competes receives a participation award, and trophies are awarded to the fastest cars. For this part of the competition, the cars may weigh no more than five ounces and, of course, that was where I was to do my job.

I had done this when I was a Cubmaster, so I remembered to bring a few supplies along. I had an Exacto knife to shave a car that was a bit overweight, fast-drying glue for emergency repairs, and a few lead weights to use when the cars were too light (the heavier the car, the faster it will roll down the track). I also had a bottle of graphite lubricant and some fine sandpaper, and I was sure I could deal with any problem that would arise.

Ideally, the boy should build the car with help from an adult, and a few of the cars actually looked as though this directive had been followed. There were also a few cars that were built completely by adults and, sadly, a few for which the boys had received no help at all. I drafted a dad to help me with the minor adjustments, and the weigh-in went along very smoothly until

Johnny and his father handed me The Car.

This was the most beautiful Pinewood Derby car I had ever seen. Unfortunately, it was a foot long and weighed about three pounds. Apparently, the boy's father had decided that the kit containing the materials to build a wooden car wasn't good enough for his son, so he put it aside and had a steel car built from scratch in a machine shop.

Instead of the little plastic wheels that used a nail as an axle, this car had machined axles, rubber tires, and wheels with ball bearings. The black paint job with the gold and red trim would have made any sports car enthusiast envious, and it was obvious that his son had played no part in designing or building it. I had to tell him that this work of art was oversized and overweight and was disqualified, and I really enjoyed doing it.

Johnny's dad wasn't very adult about my decision. He went on and on about how much effort he had put into this car and how much it had cost. He didn't have a clue, though, that he had missed the whole point. He had ignored his son and taken advantage of the Cub Scouts to build himself a nifty little toy. I'm sure he would have gloated and run around slapping high fives when his car outraced the ones built by eight-, nine-, and ten-year-old boys. I finally yielded and said he could display his car by running it down the track. I had trouble suppressing a smile when it wouldn't roll because it was built with so little bottom clearance it couldn't even clear the guide strip.

Once the races were completed, everyone knew who the overall winner was, but the judges needed a little time to calculate the finish times for the rest of the boys. During this pause in the action, refreshments were served and the boys had the opportunity to vote for the appearance awards. Since the pack leaders wanted every boy to win something, there were probably fifteen or twenty different categories.

The boys showed wisdom and judgment far beyond their years when The Car received only one vote in both the Most Unusual and Best-Looking categories. As everyone was leaving to go home, the car's owner came over to me and told me that he hadn't realized he was supposed to use the kit to build the car and that his son was supposed to be involved.

I was just about to say something I would have later regretted when I changed my mind and just wished him better luck next year.

Chapter 49.   Did I Say That?

I really enjoyed being a Unit Commissioner, and at first the position allowed me to have a lot of free time. That was soon going to change.

We were at a District Camp-O-Ree when our Council Commissioner, Bill Terrinoni, came over and said he wanted to talk to me. After fifteen years of working with him I have now learned what he means whenever he says that, but at that time I barely knew him, so I listened.

We chatted briefly about what I was doing as a Unit Commissioner and then he asked me whether I would accept the position of District Commissioner. I was really shocked because I had been in my post for only eighteen months and I told him so. I also told him that I had no administrative experience and I wasn't sure I could run the District Commissioner's staff.

"Surely there are many commissioners in our district who are more qualified than I am," I told him. Why don't you ask them?"

"I did," he answered, "but they all said no."

"Exactly how many did you ask?"

He hesitated for a minute or two and then

told me that six people had turned him down. I thought about this new challenge and then, figuring that since they wouldn't expect too much from a seventh choice, I took the job.

As a Unit Commissioner I kept in touch with the units I was responsible for and attended monthly Commissioner meetings. I had never been particularly interested in the administration of a district, but now I had to learn. It wasn't very long before I found out why the other six people had said no to Bill. Our district was in a shambles and was very close to being broken up and absorbed by the surrounding districts. Bill must have figured I couldn't make things any worse than they were.

One of the ways a Scout district is evaluated is by the health of its packs, troops, and posts, and we were terminally ill. We were losing units at a record pace, and reversing that trend became my first priority. I met with our District Executive, Jeff Purdy (the paid professional), and together we resolved not to lose another unit.

Jeff and I spent many long hours working with my staff and with troubled units, and slowly but surely things began to turn around. The long hours of hard work paid off and we actually made it to the end of the year with all units still in place.

We were well into our second year when a Cub Scout pack came very close to disbanding. Jeff and I went to meet with the parents to try to salvage it. There were only about 10 boys left in the pack and there were no leaders.

We tried for over an hour to get some of the parents to step up and help, but all we could get was a treasurer and one lady who said she would serve on the committee. I can usually keep my cool, but something happened at this meeting and I lost it.

"Okay," I said. "None of you have any time to give your sons. But if you look outside this building you'll find the drug dealers and gangbangers waiting to devote all their time to your kids. They are ready to teach your boys everything they will need to know to ruin their lives. So why don't you just help them out by taking your kids outside and introducing them? Then you won't have to spend any time at all with them."

As I stopped to catch my breath, I looked toward the back of the room, and there was Jeff in very obvious distress. His face was a strange color I had never seen before. I think it was

176

somewhere between green and purple, and I wondered whether I had gone just a bit too far. It was really quiet in the room and I just stood there and waited to see what would happen next.

The silence lasted for what seemed like an hour, although it was probably just three or four minutes, and then one man got up and walked over to the chart that listed the positions that needed to be filled. Without a word, he wrote his name in the Cubmaster slot and then sat down.

One by one, all the parents in the room walked up to the chart, and in just a few minutes every position was filled. Jeff, whose face had returned to its normal color, took over to handle the administrative stuff that needed to be done, and I just sat down in the back of the room to watch. It wasn't long before everything was finished and everyone had left.

I invited Jeff to join me for a cup of coffee to celebrate our success, and he accepted. He arrived at the restaurant before I did and was waiting for me in a booth. I was pretty pleased with what we had accomplished, but as I sat down I thought I saw a slight hint of greenish purple on his face.

He was mumbling under his breath and I

could just make out that he was saying, "I can't believe you said that." And then he gave me the kind of look you don't want to get from someone who is a foot taller than you and outweighs you by seventy-five pounds.

"Never do that again," he said, and I had no trouble at all understanding him or complying with his directive–even if I didn't agree with him.

Chapter 50.   Vigil Honor

One of the meetings I had to attend as District Commissioner was our monthly District Committee meeting. During the October meeting, Betty Wurster came over to me and asked whether I was going to the Order of the Arrow banquet in December. I told her that I had not yet decided but was thinking about it. She told me that John Logan, our District Chairman, was going to receive the Vigil Honor and it would be nice to have as many district people as possible at the banquet. So I promised to attend.

The Order of the Arrow Vigil Honor is something that an individual cannot work for and earn. Every year a committee recognizes adults who they feel are deserving, but the final selection is made by the boys in the O-A and there is a formal recognition ceremony at the December banquet. John was a very hard worker, and I was happy to learn that he would be one of the recipients.

About a week later I received a phone call from Bill Terrinoni, asking whether I would be at the banquet. I assured him that I would be there and, although I thought it was strange to have so many people asking whether I was going, never gave it another thought.

As I was getting ready to leave for the banquet, Dawn seemed much more curious than normal. She felt out of place at these Scouting functions and I had stopped inviting her a long time ago. I had a strange feeling that she wanted me to ask her to go along but, certain that I was mistaken, went on to the banquet alone.

At the banquet hall, Betty came over and told me that she had saved a seat for me at her table.

"Where's John?" I asked her. "I don't see him anywhere."

"He's over in that far corner with some of his other friends," she replied and quickly changed the subject.

Dinner was served and was followed by the inevitable speeches and the evening's entertainment. As the time came to announce the names of those selected to receive the Vigil Honor, I still didn't see John anywhere in the room.

The boys who were to be honored were called first and they lined up at the front of the room. As they began naming the adults, one of the descriptions sounded awfully familiar and then my name was called. As I rose to go up to the front, Betty had an ear-to-ear grin on her face and suddenly all the strange events of the last two months made sense.

She had even called Dawn and invited her. Unfortunately, there was no way Dawn could ask to go without making me very suspicious about the reason for her sudden change in attitude.

Once you are selected for the Vigil Honor there are certain rituals you must observe, and it is not appropriate for me to describe them in this book. Suffice it to say that Arrowmen who have been awarded the honor know what the rituals are, other Order of the Arrow members have something to look forward to, and parents should take the opportunity to become volunteers in the Boy Scouts of America and some day they may have the opportunity to find out for themselves.

Epilogue

During the summer of 1988 two other Scouters and I met to develop a plan for an advanced training program for Scout leaders. This work took nearly a full year to complete and ultimately led to the development of the Lord Baden-Powell University of Scouting.

After serving in numerous capacities on the LBPU steering committee, I became Dean of the University in the spring of 2002. I left that position in March 2005, and even though I continue to serve as Dean Emeritus, I look back wistfully on the time I spent working with boys and watching them mature and grow into fine young men.

There is a church, not far from where I live, that sponsors both a Cub Scout pack and a Boy Scout troop. I think I'll call them to see whether they could use the services of a Scouter with a few years' experience.

I know I'm a little older and slower than most leaders, but why not give it a try? After all, it's only an hour a week.